KU-789-146

Number Textbook

Peter Patilla
Ann Montague-Smith
Paul Broadbent

Addison Wesley Longman Limited

Edinburgh Gate, Harlow, Essex, CM20, 2JE, England and
Associated Companies throughout the World

First published 1996

Designed and typeset by Gecko Design Limited
Illustrations by Gecko Ltd, Madeleine Baker, Phil Burrows, Roger Fereday, Tania Hurt-Newton, Andrew McLaughlin, Peter Richardson
Picture Researcher, Valerie Mulcahy

We are grateful to the following for permission to reproduce photographs:

Gareth Boden, page 17; Brue Coleman Limited, pages 62 left (Normal Tomalin), 63 left (Steve Alden); Tony Stone Images, page 62 right (David Ball); Zeta, page 63 right.

We are grateful to Roger Ascham Primary School for their invaluable help in creating the photography for this book.

The publisher's policy is to use paper manufactured from sustainable forests.

Printed in Hong Kong

CONTENTS

Sta[illegible]

A Copy the [illegible]
Replace the stars with numbers.

1. × = 15
2. × = 28
3. × = 27
4. × = 60
5. × = 35
6. × = 25

B Look at the example.
Copy the stars, then write different divide sums on the points.

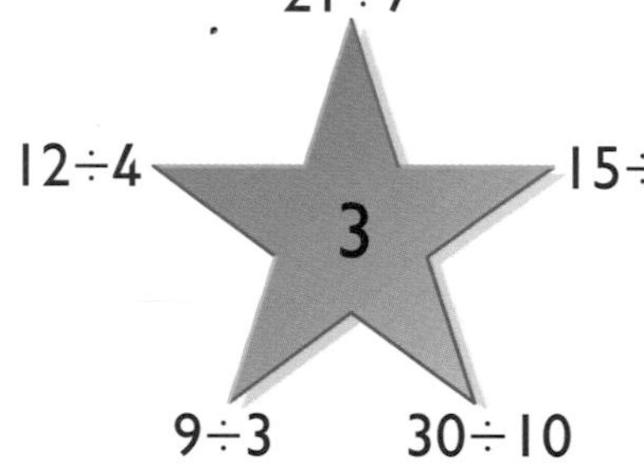

21÷7
12÷4
15÷5
3
9÷3
30÷10

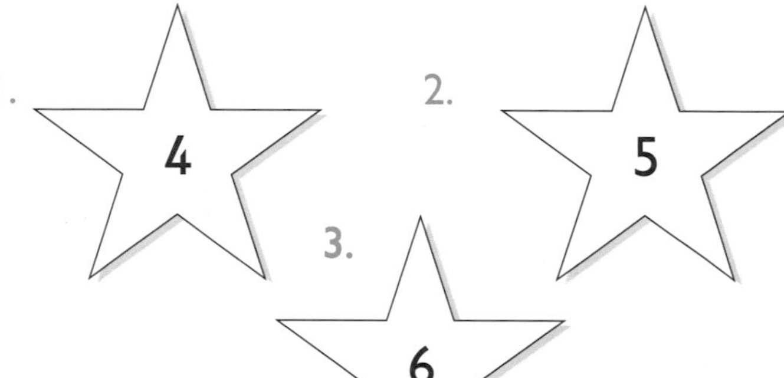

1.
4
2.
5
3.
6

Helpful hint
Write the digits on small pieces of paper.

C Each star is a consecutive number.
Copy and replace the stars with numbers.

1. ★ + ★ + ★ = 24
2. ★ + ★ + ★ + ★ = 26
3. ★ + ★ + ★ + ★ + ★ = 25

Challenge

Copy this star.
Write the digits 1 to 9 in the circles.
Each line must have the same total.

Unit 1 Maths journeys

A Copy and complete the signs.

1.
126
130
134
138
2.
151
146
141
136
3.
123
132
141
150

B Write the distance you think each car has travelled.

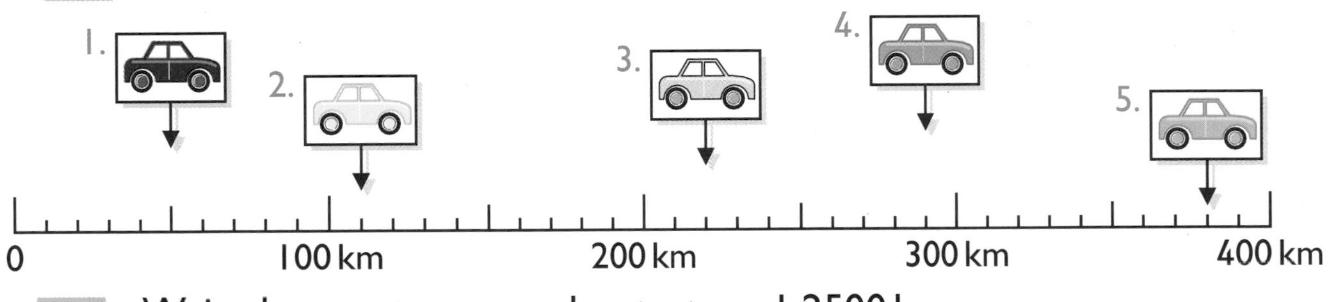

1.
2.
3.
4.
5.
0
100 km
200 km
300 km
400 km

C Write how many more km to travel 2500 km.

1.

02350

2.

02175

3.

01550

4.

01050

A Write these as numbers.

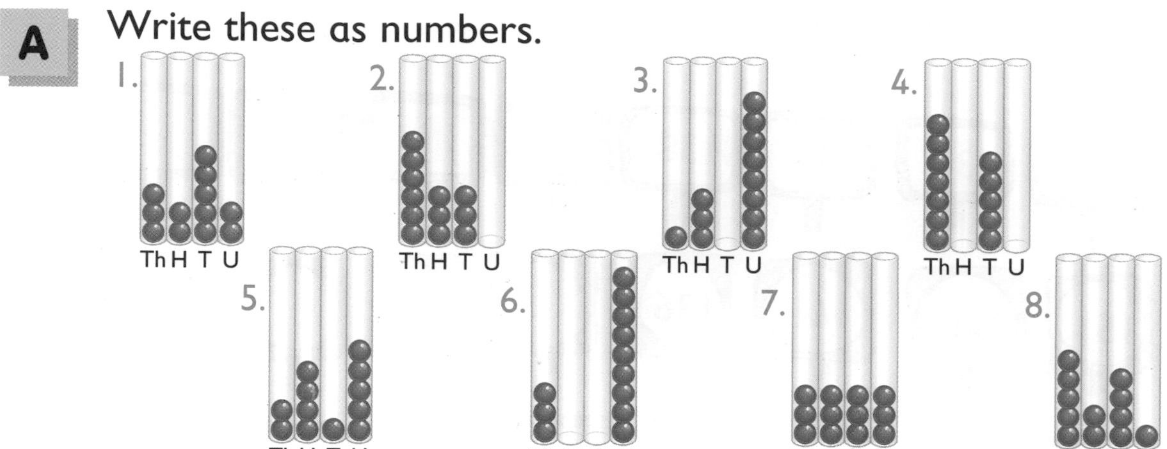

1.
ThH T U
2.
ThH T U
3.
ThH T U
4.
ThH T U
5.
ThH T U
6.
ThH T U
7.
ThH T U
8.
ThH T U

B Write these numbers in order.

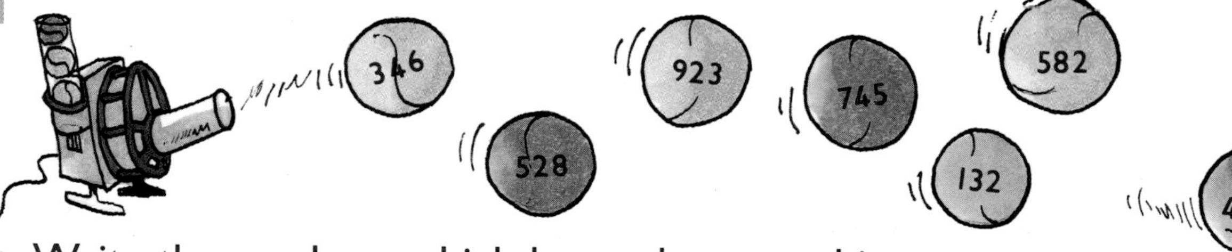

346
528
923
745
582
132
457

C Write the numbers which leave these machines.

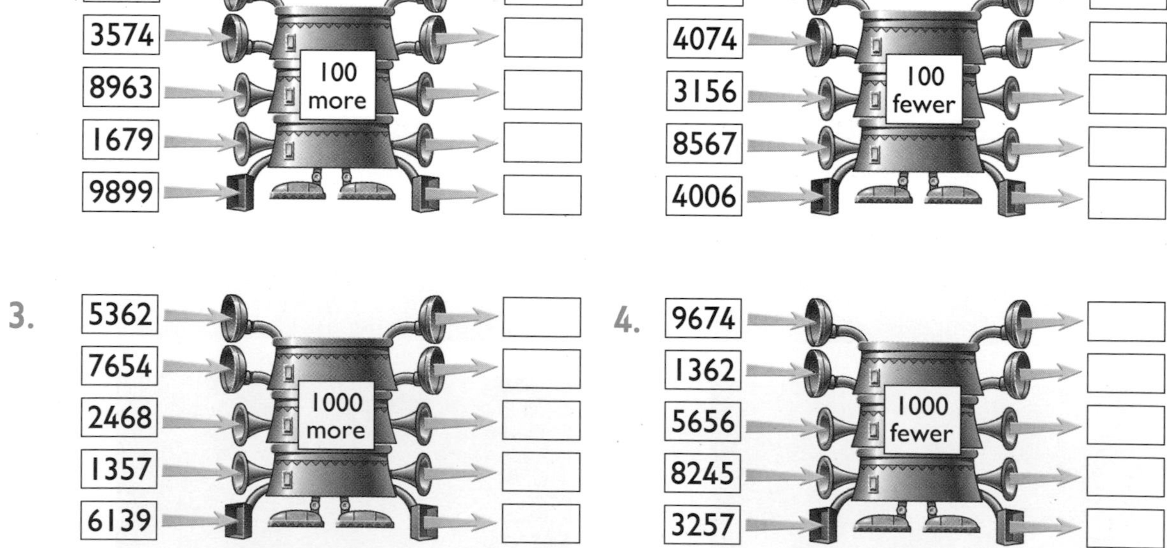

1.
8362
3574
8963
1679
9899
100 more
2.
9346
4074
3156
8567
4006
100 fewer
3.
5362
7654
2468
1357
6139
1000 more
4.
9674
1362
5656
8245
3257
1000 fewer

Thousands

A Write in words the value of the digit in the square.

1. 53[6]5 2. [5]365 3. 5[3]65 4. 536[5]
5. 7[4]63 6. 94[5]1 7. 852[1] 8. [6]531

B The letter k stands for thousands.
17k = 17000.

Write these numbers in full:

1. 5k 2. 25k 3. 100k 4. 1000k

C **20k expected to queue for tickets for final**

Copy and complete this table of attendances at the tennis tournament.

	Actual attendance	Attendance to the nearest k
Monday	16843	
Tuesday	12378	
Wednesday	12506	
Thursday	13043	
Friday	18487	
Saturday	20592	

Adding

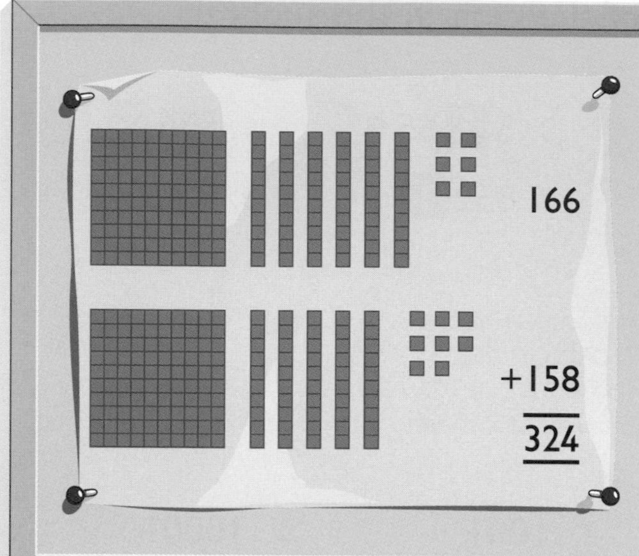
166
+158
324

Add the units.
Change units for tens.
Add the tens.
Change tens for hundreds.
Add the hundreds.

A You can use place value apparatus.

1.
```
  346
+ 239
```

2.
```
  456
+ 372
```

3.
```
  396
+ 257
```

4.
```
  286
+ 538
```

5.
```
  405
  396
+  27
```

6.
```
  615
  165
+ 152
```

7.
```
  723
   46
+ 187
```

8.
```
  389
  278
+ 197
```

B Write out these sums and answer them.

1. 346 + 271
2. 646 + 329
3. 195 + 767
4. 148 + 362 + 258
5. 562 + 39 + 328
6. 319 + 62 + 413
7. 156 + 327 + 59
8. 64 + 73 + 816

Game totals

A Write the totals for each player.

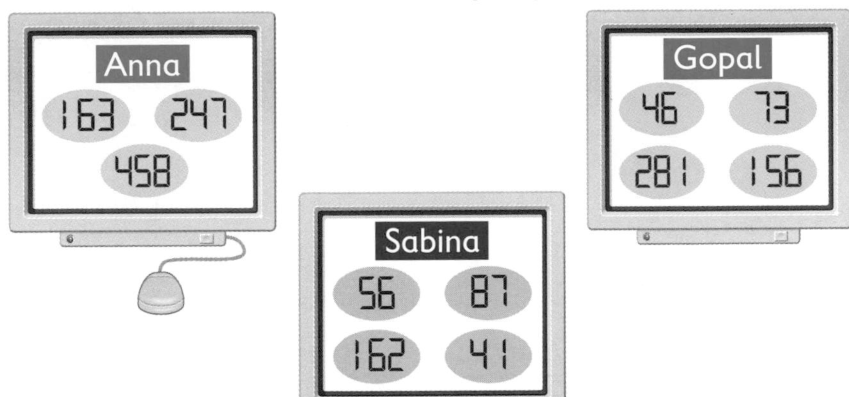
Anna
163 247
458
Sabina
56 87
162 41
Gopal
46 73
281 156

Guy
309 58
577

B These are the scores after three games.

1. Who scored the largest total?
2. Who had the smallest total?
3. Find the total score for Anna.
4. Who scored a total of 620?
5. Who scored nearest to 750?

Game	1	2	3
Anna	156	253	354
Sabina	306	219	95
Gopal	237	245	476
Guy	146	182	96

C Write different scores to total 564 for each player.

Anna
* * *
* * *
* * *
5 6 4

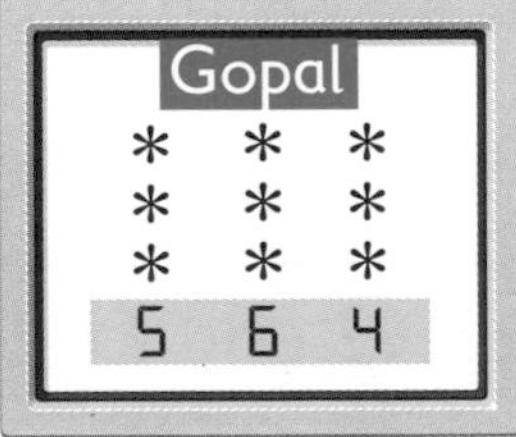
Gopal
* * *
* * *
* * *
5 6 4

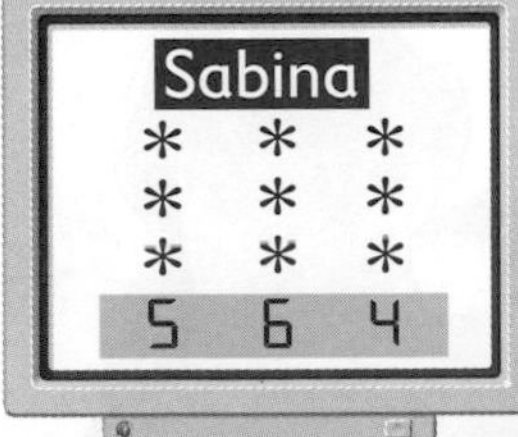
Sabina
* * *
* * *
* * *
5 6 4

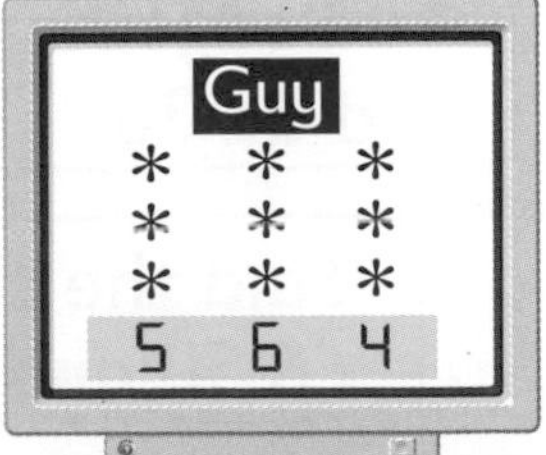
Guy
* * *
* * *
* * *
5 6 4

Money totals

A Write how much in each bag.

1.

£5
20p
2p
2p
20p
20p

2. £1 50p 20p £1.70

3.

£1
50p
10p
£1
10p

4. 50p £1 20p £1 5p 50p 1p 1p

5. £5 £1 2p £1 £1 10p £1 5p 10p

B

$$\begin{array}{r} £3.56 \\ +\ £4.69 \\ \hline £8.25 \end{array}$$

Add the pence.
Change pence for pounds.
Add the pounds.

1. $\begin{array}{r} £2.25 \\ +\ £3.45 \\ \hline \end{array}$ _____
2. $\begin{array}{r} £6.27 \\ +\ £2.85 \\ \hline \end{array}$ _____
3. $\begin{array}{r} £3.62 \\ +\ £5.75 \\ \hline \end{array}$ _____
4. $\begin{array}{r} £2.48 \\ +\ £5.35 \\ \hline \end{array}$ _____
5. $\begin{array}{r} £5.49 \\ +\ £3.75 \\ \hline \end{array}$ _____
6. $\begin{array}{r} £1.97 \\ +\ £3.79 \\ \hline \end{array}$ _____
7. $\begin{array}{r} £0.96 \\ +\ £8.37 \\ \hline \end{array}$ _____
8. $\begin{array}{r} £4.31 \\ +\ £5.96 \\ \hline \end{array}$ _____

C Write the answers to these.

1. Total £3·42 and £1·27.
2. Add together £4·76 and £2·36.
3. Find the sum of £2·34, £6·50 and £1·37.
4. Add £1·95 to £6·73.
5. Find the total of £3·26, £1·87 and £2·95.

Unit 1 Number problems

A Write the total cost and total weight for each basket.

1.

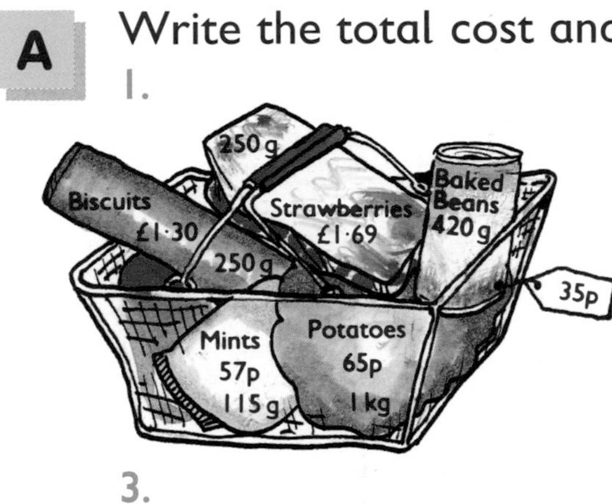

250 g
Biscuits
£1·30
Strawberries
£1·69
250 g
Baked Beans
420 g
35p
Mints
57p
115 g
Potatoes
65p
1 kg

2.

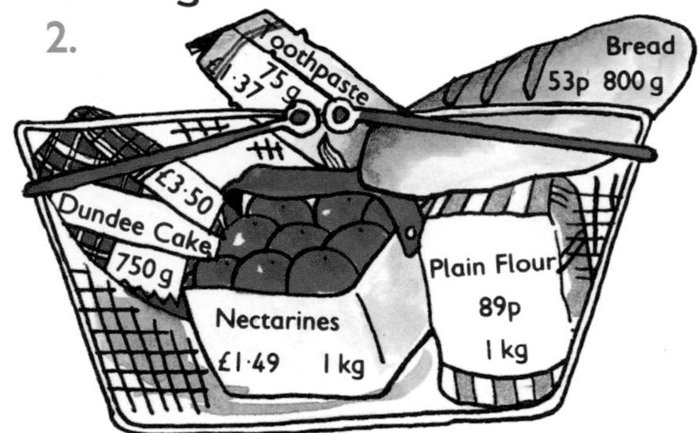

Toothpaste
75 g
£1·37
Bread
53p 800 g
£3·50
Dundee Cake
750 g
Nectarines
£1·49 1 kg
Plain Flour
89p
1 kg

3.

£1·30
Cornflakes
750 g
Crisps
£1·29
150 g
Sliced ham
£1·63
250 g
Lentils
88p
500 g

4.

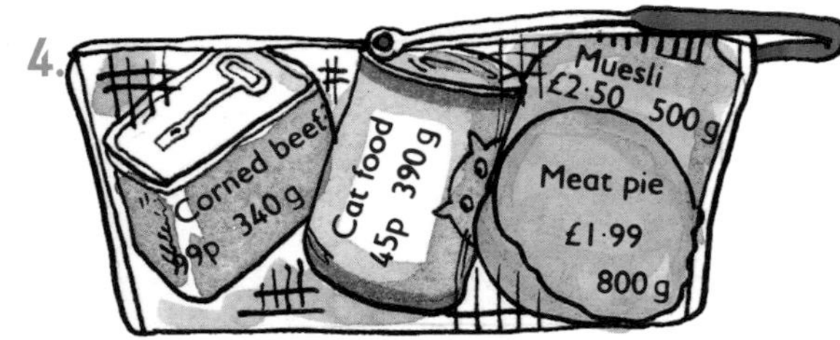

Corned beef
340 g
Cat food
45p 390 g
Muesli
£2·50 500 g
Meat pie
£1·99
800 g

B Answer these in sentences.

1. Which till had the most customers?
2. Find the total number of customers for Saturday.
3. On which day was the shop the busiest?
4. On which day did the shop have fewest customers? Why do you think this is?

Number of customers at the mini-market

	Till 1	Till 2	Till 3
Monday	110	129	131
Tuesday	176	114	205
Wednesday	89	37	64
Thursday	256	276	249
Friday	195	118	174
Saturday	163	145	175

Van deliveries

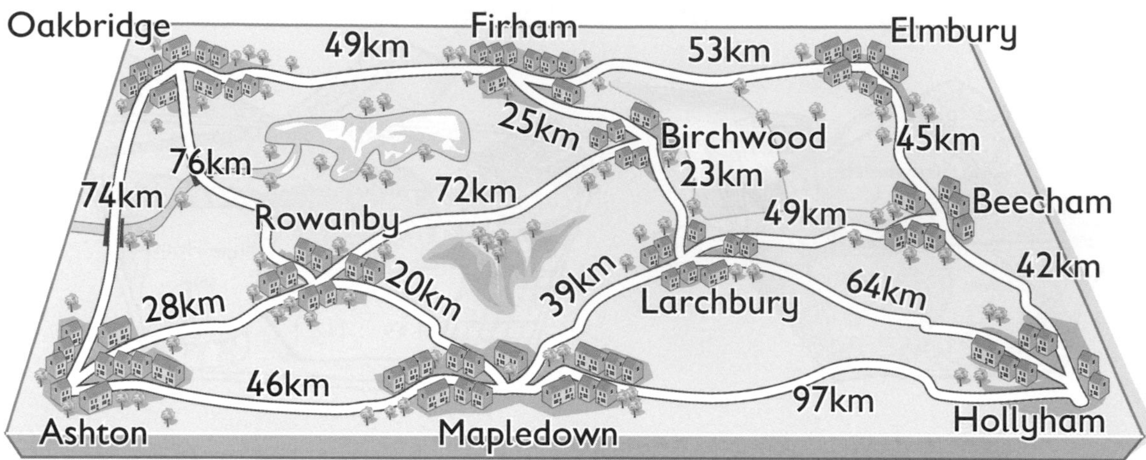
Oakbridge
49km
Firham
53km
Elmbury
25km
Birchwood
45km
76km
23km
74km
72km
Rowanby
49km
Beecham
20km
39km
42km
28km
Larchbury
64km
46km
97km
Ashton
Mapledown
Hollyham

Mr Brown is a van driver who lives in Oakbridge. These are his deliveries for the week.

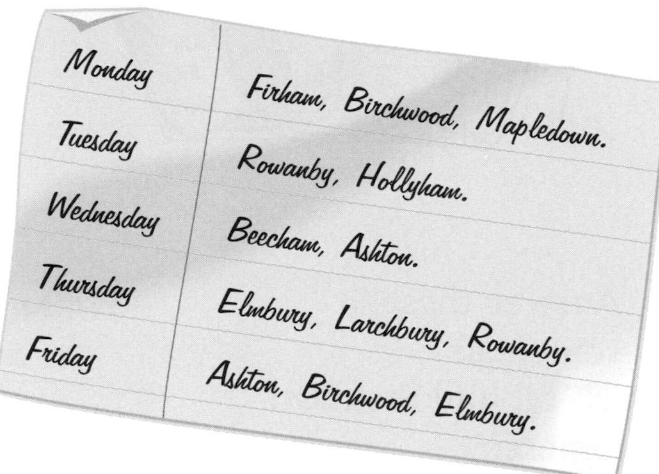

Monday	Firham, Birchwood, Mapledown.
Tuesday	Rowanby, Hollyham.
Wednesday	Beecham, Ashton.
Thursday	Elmbury, Larchbury, Rowanby.
Friday	Ashton, Birchwood, Elmbury.

A Each day he starts and finishes in Oakbridge and travels by the shortest route.

Write how far he travels on each day of the week.

B These are his fuel bills.

BIRCHWOOD SERVICES
30 litres at 53p £15.90

Ashton Petrol
25 litres at 54p
£13.50

ELMBURY GARAGE
33 litres at 52p
£17.16

Write the total cost of the fuel.

Unit 1 Number quiz

A

Write which answer fits the clue.

5174

1. This number is 1 fewer than 100 000.
2. This number is twice 8965.
3. These numbers are palindromes.
   They read the same forwards and backwards.

3875

4. This number has
   - 4 digits
   - the sums of its digits is 23.

17930

5. This number has
   - 4 digits
   - the tens digit is 8.

96169

6. This number is the sum of 1099 and 4075.

49654

3784

Challenge

Use a calculator.

1. Find the largest number you can display.
2. Find the largest number you can display whose digits total 50.
3. Find three other numbers you can display whose digits total 50.

Magic squares

In a magic square rows, columns and diagonals have the same total.

4	3	8
9	5	1
2	7	6

Did You Know?

Magic squares were probably discovered in 2200 BC by Emperor Yu. They were called Lo-Shu. Lo-Shu used dot patterns.

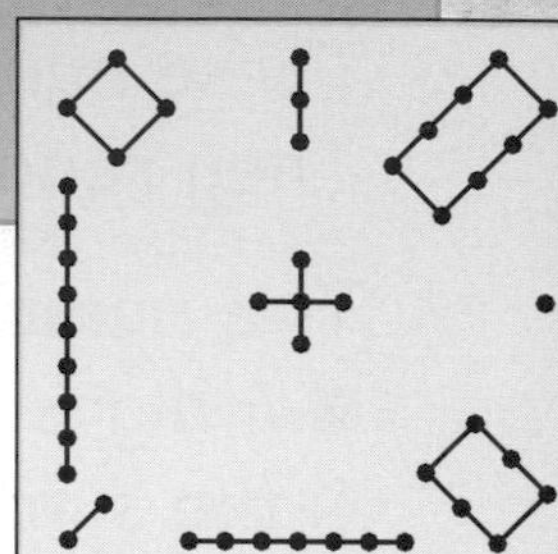

A Copy and complete these magic squares.

1.

	1	
		7
		2

2.

	7	
1		
		4

3.

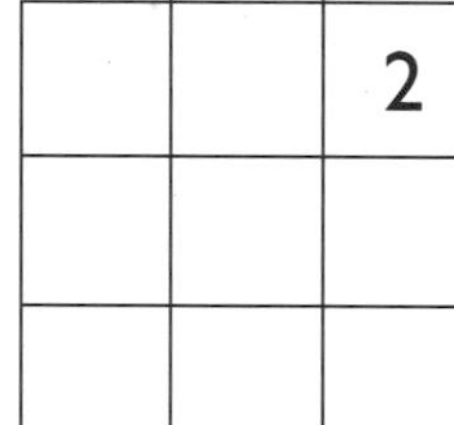

		2

4.

1			4
12			
	11		
13		3	16

B Find out if a magic square is still magic if you:

1. Add 5 to each number.
2. Double each number.

Draw magic squares to show what you have found out.

C Hollow magic squares do not have a middle number.

5	2	6
7		3
1	8	4

Find other hollow magic squares which use these numbers:

1
2
3
4
5
6
7
8

D In the 18th century a Swiss mathematician called Leonard Euler designed this magic square which used the numbers 1 to 64.

18	63	16	33	50	31	48	1
35	14	19	62	3	46	51	30
64	17	34	15	32	49	2	47
13	36	61	20	45	4	29	52
60	21	40	9	56	25	44	5
37	12	57	24	41	8	53	28
22	59	10	39	26	55	6	43
11	38	23	58	7	42	27	54

What is special about the totals in:
- each row?
- each column?
- each of the four squares?

Explore other totals and write about what you have found out.

Taking away

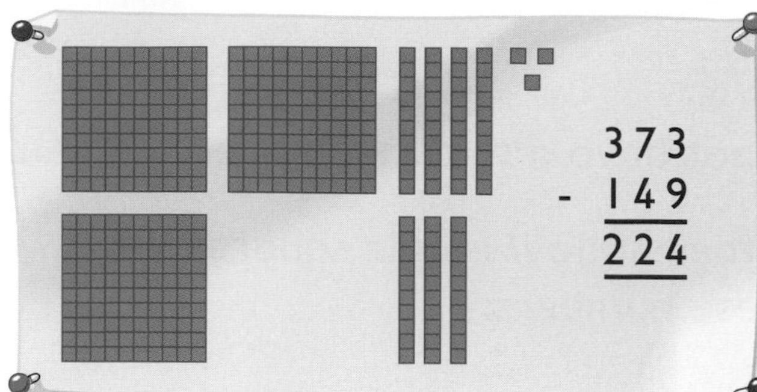
373
- 149
224

Subtract the units.
Change a hundred for tens.
Subtract the tens.
Subtract the hundreds.

A You can use apparatus.

1. 475 − 238
2. 526 − 318
3. 986 − 249
4. 845 − 306
5. 435 − 217
6. 777 − 549
7. 390 − 276
8. 615 − 308

Subtract the units.
Change a hundred for tens.
Subtract the tens.
Subtract the hundreds.

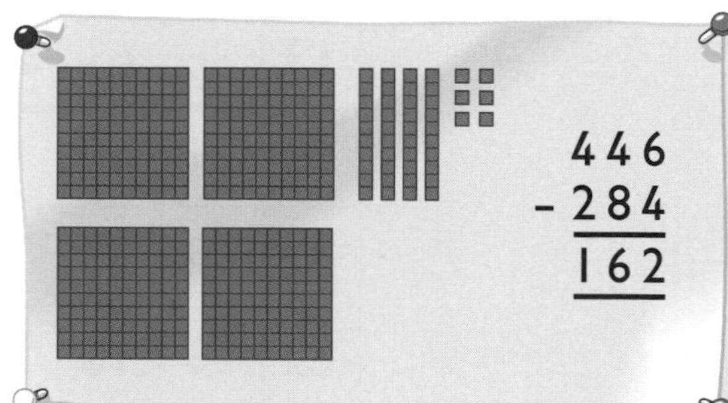
446
- 284
162

B

1. 476 − 285
2. 519 − 344
3. 304 − 191
4. 964 − 390
5. 826 − 674
6. 737 − 256
7. 658 − 467
8. 439 − 148

Unit 2 Recycling

A Which ones can you do in your head?
Write the answers.
Copy and complete the others.

1.
923
− 632
2.
456
− 372
3.
789
− 359
4.
654
− 348
5.
846
− 339
6.
874
− 783
7.
629
− 437
8.
467
− 258

B

1. How many more cans were collected in January than February?
2. What is the difference between the collections in April and May?
3. What is the difference between the largest and smallest totals?
4. How many more cans are needed to reach their target?

COLLECTING CANS FOR RECYCLING

TARGET 3000 CANS

Month	Cans Collected
January	673
February	459
March	585
April	137
May	469

ALUMINIUM
DRINKS
CANS ONLY.
Test All Cans
With a Magnet.
If They're Aluminium,
The Magnet
Won't Stick.

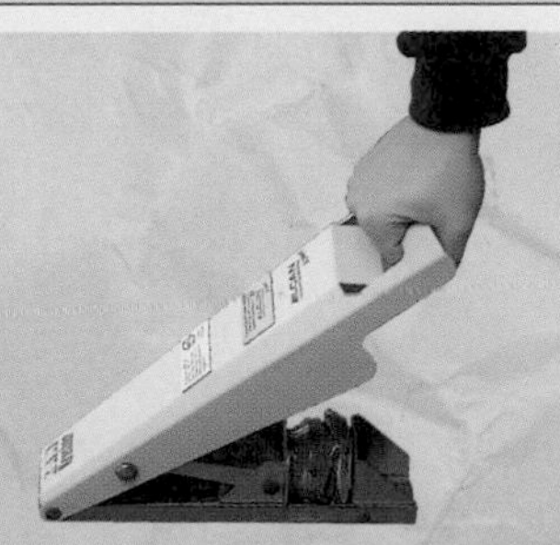

More taking away

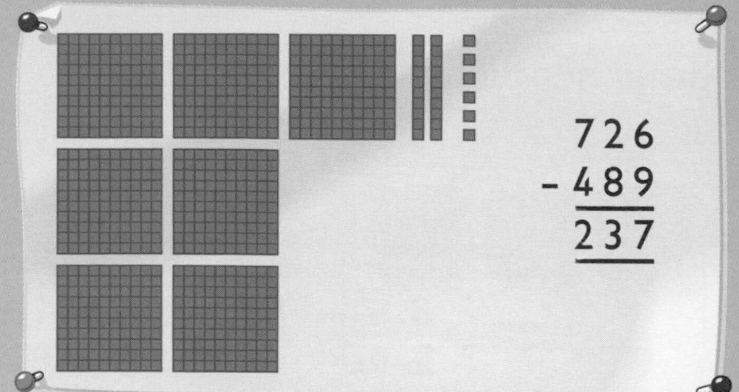
726
- 489
237

Change a ten for units.
Subtract the units.
Change a hundred for tens.
Subtract the tens.
Subtract the hundreds.

A

You can use apparatus.

1. 546 − 379	2. 643 − 344	3. 726 − 148	4. 838 − 299
5. 432 − 187	6. 911 − 156	7. 567 − 388	8. 427 − 149

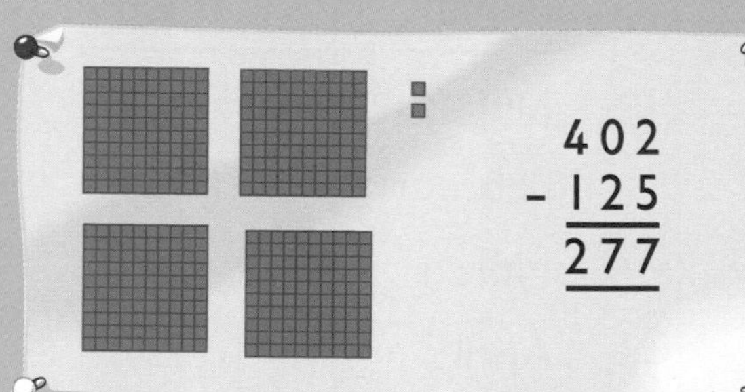
402
- 125
277

Change a hundred for tens.
Change a ten for units.
Subtract the units.
Subtract the tens.
Subtract the hundreds.

B

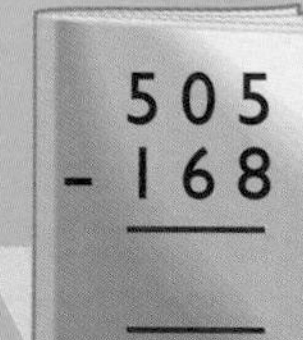

1. 505 − 168	2. 604 − 337	3. 706 − 549	4. 302 − 193
5. 803 − 654	6. 901 − 257	7. 804 − 237	8. 600 − 198

Charity week

A Choose those you can do in your head.
Write the answers.
Copy and complete the others.

1. 503 − 292
2. 634 − 158
3. 746 − 359
4. 801 − 399
5. 721 − 345
6. 478 − 299
7. 705 − 439
8. 608 − 439
B
Grace
NATALIE
PHIL

Each collector has 750 stickers to sell.

1. Copy and complete the table.
2. How many stickers did Natalie have left at the end of the day?
3. How many more did Phil sell than Grace?
4. How many more did Grace sell in the afternoon than in the morning?

	Stickers sold		
	Morning	Afternoon	Total
Grace	229		618
Natalie	346		601
Phil	191		730

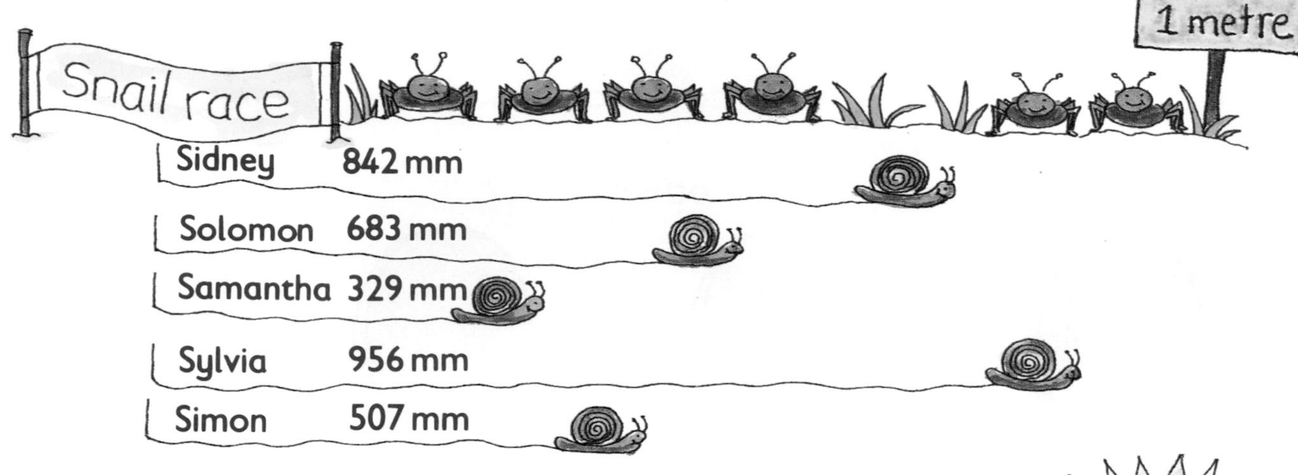

1 metre
Snail race
Sidney 842 mm
Solomon 683 mm
Samantha 329 mm
Sylvia 956 mm
Simon 507 mm

A The distances the snails had travelled in 10 minutes were measured in millimetres.

1. How far ahead of Sidney was Sylvia?
2. How far behind Simon was Samantha?
3. How much further did Solomon need to travel to pass the finishing line?
4. What was the difference between the distances Sidney and Solomon had travelled?

Sunflower climbing

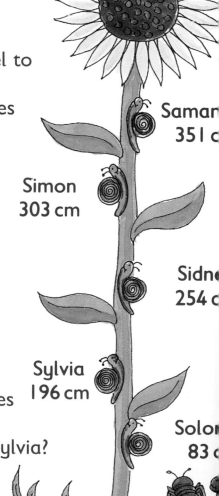

B The snails had a sunflower climbing race.

1. How much further did Simon climb than Sylvia?
2. What was the difference between the highest and lowest heights climbed?
3. What was the difference between the distances Sidney and Samantha climbed?
4. How much further did Samantha climb than Sylvia?

Simon
303 cm
Sylvia
196 cm

Saman
351 c

Sidn
254 c

Solo
83 c

C

Number of hayseeds pulled
293
Sylvia
516
Solomon
500
Samantha
340
Sidney
548
Simon

1. How many more did Solomon pull than Sidney?
2. How many fewer did Sidney pull than Simon?
3. How many more seeds did Sidney need to equal Samantha?
4. What was the difference between the highest and fewest number of seeds?

D

Distance travelled in 1 minute	
Samantha	238 metres
Sidney	359 metres
Simon	504 metres
Sylvia	396 metres
Solomon	451 metres

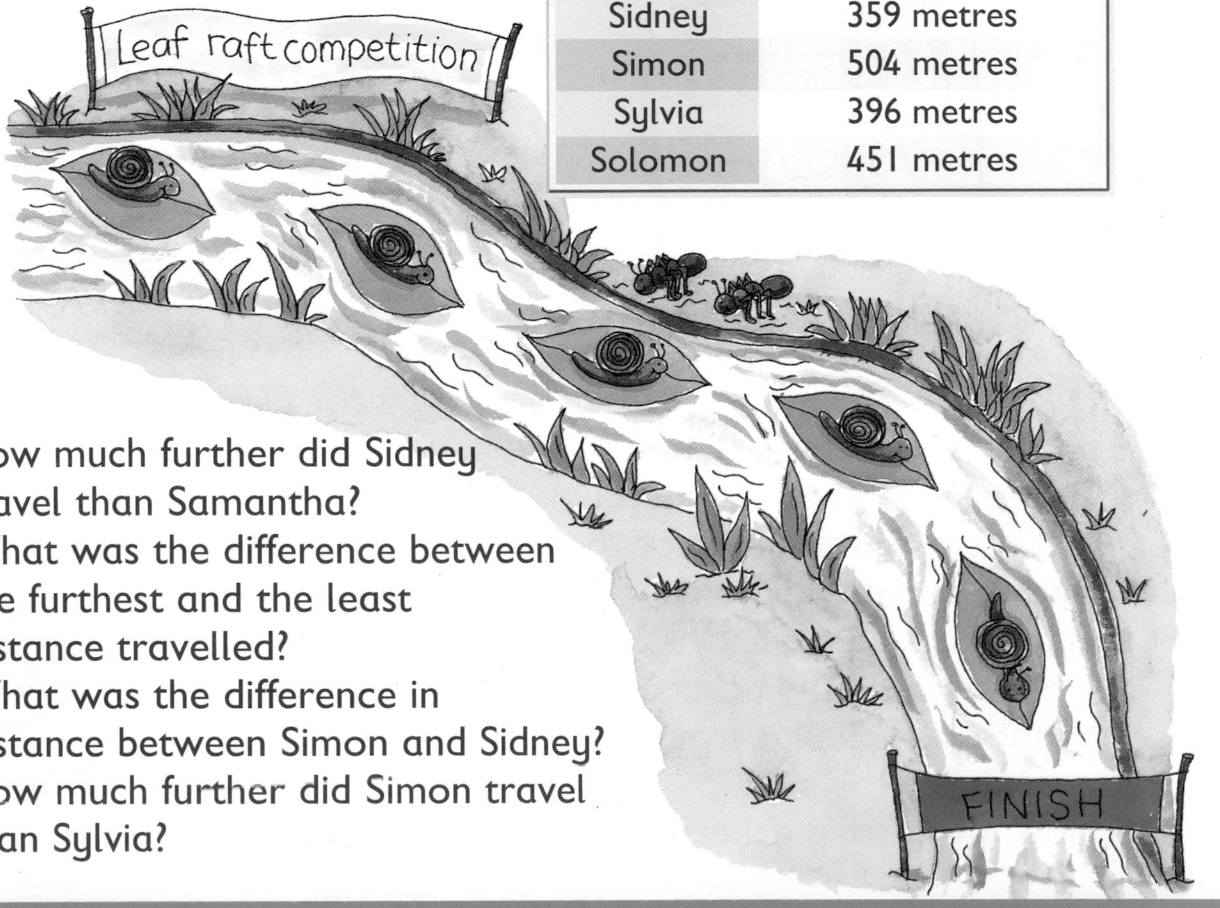

Leaf raft competition

FINISH

1. How much further did Sidney travel than Samantha?
2. What was the difference between the furthest and the least distance travelled?
3. What was the difference in distance between Simon and Sidney?
4. How much further did Simon travel than Sylvia?

THEATRE
SEAT C19
£9.00
PROGRAMME
HENRY V
SWIMMING
£1·20
THEME PARK
£9.00
CINEMA
£5·00
MUSEUM
ENTRANCE
£2·00
POPCORN
THE BIG
DIPPER
MUSEUM
GUIDE
SAFARI
PARK
£6·00
Rules—
• Do not leave your car
• Do not feed animals
• Do not sound horn
TRAIN TICKETS
ADULTS £3·00
CHILDREN £1·50
Train
Timetable

Our day out

Write the answers in sentences.

1. How many cinema tickets can be bought for £40?
2. Find the cost of five theatre tickets.
3. Four people go to the Museum. What change will there be from £10 for the tickets?
4. Two adults and three children go to the Safari Park by train. How much do the tickets and train fares total?
5. What is the change from £5 for three swimming pool tickets?
6. How many train tickets can be bought for £24?

THE SEA PEARL TAKEAWAY

MENU

Soup	£1·24
Spare ribs	£3·46
Prawncrackers	87p
Spring rolls	£1·24
Beansprouts	£1·16
Fried rice	99p
Chop suey	£2·78
Chow mein	£3·09
Foo yung	£4·17
Sweet & sour pork	£3·95
Sea Pearl special	£4·57
Pineapple fritter	£1·13

Eating out

Write the answers.

1. Find the total cost of soup, spring rolls and Sea Pearl special.
2. What is the difference in price between Sea Pearl special and chop suey?
3. How much more expensive is sweet and sour pork than fried rice?
4. Do foo yung and spare ribs cost more than Sea Pearl special and chow mein?
5. How much change will you get from £9 if you buy foo yung, spring rolls, bean sprouts and a pineapple fritter?

Challenge

You have £10 to spend. Choose from the menu and write a bill.

When part of the problem is in brackets, you work out the brackets part first.

15 – (12 – 4)
15 – 8 = 7

A Copy and answer these.

1. (17 – 3) + 4
2. 15 – (7 – 2)
3. (13 – 5) – 4
4. 16 + (8 – 3)
5. 14 – (7 + 3)
6. (8 + 6) – 5

B Copy the sums.
Draw brackets to make each answer 12.

1. 19 – 12 – 5
2. 16 – 10 – 6
3. 22 – 5 + 5
4. 6 + 13 – 7
5. 24 – 6 – 6
6. 20 – 10 – 2

C Copy the sums.
Replace the ● with numbers.

1. (● × 4) – 1 = 11
2. 10 – (● × 3) = 4
3. (● × 2) + (● × 3) = 17
4. (● × 5) – (● × 4) = 10
5. 12 ÷ (● × 2) = 2
6. (● × 5) ÷ 2 = 10

Unit 3 Multiplying machines

A  Copy and complete this chart.

X	0	1	2	3	4	5	6	7	8	9	10
6						30					60
7			14				42				
8		8							64		
9								63			

B Write the numbers which leave each machine.

1. 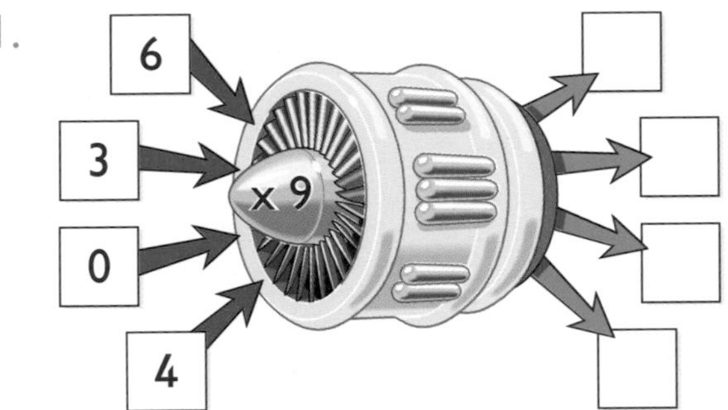
6
3
0
4
x 9

2. 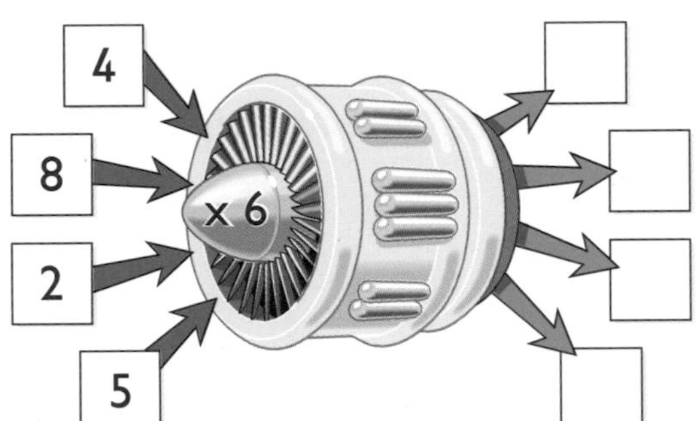
4
8
2
5
x 6

3. 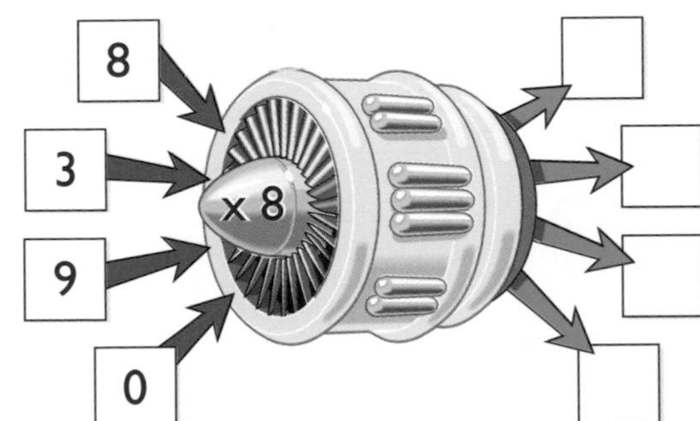
8
3
9
0
x 8

4. 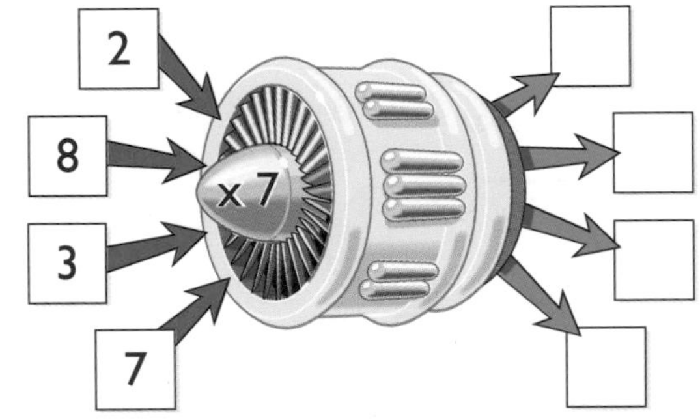
2
8
3
7
x 7

C Find the missing numbers to complete these multiplication facts.

1. ☐ × 4 = 32
2. 7 × ☐ = 35
3. 5 × 8 = ☐
4. 9 × ☐ = 81
5. ☐ × ☐ = 63
6. ☐ × 7 = 70

Multiplication patterns

Unit 3

A Here are some rectangle patterns.
Write each as a multiplication fact.

1.
3 x 6 =
6 x 3 =

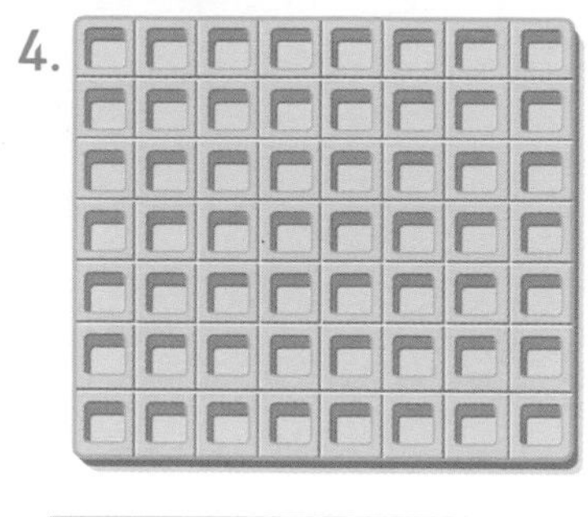
4.

6.

7.

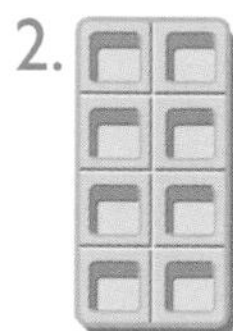
2.

3.

5.

B Draw each number as a rectangle pattern.
Write the multiplication fact.

1. 27
2. 30
3. 45
4. 14
5. 35
6. 48

3 x 4 = 12

C These are part of a table square.
Copy them and write the missing numbers.

1.
6
14
24
32
2.
21
35
32
3.
12
21
16
Maple Syrup
4.
49
64
81

Missing numbers

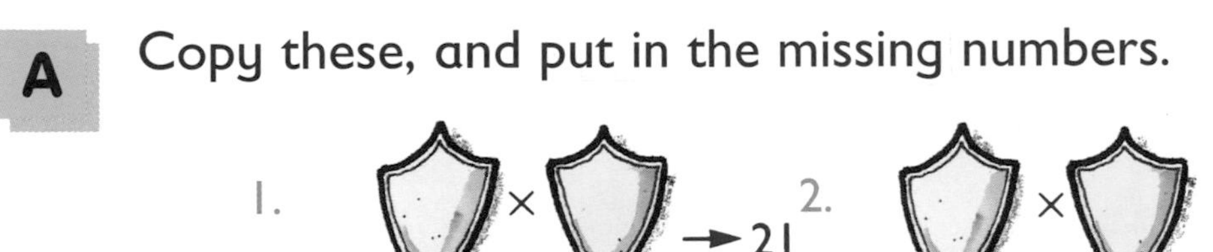

A Copy these, and put in the missing numbers.

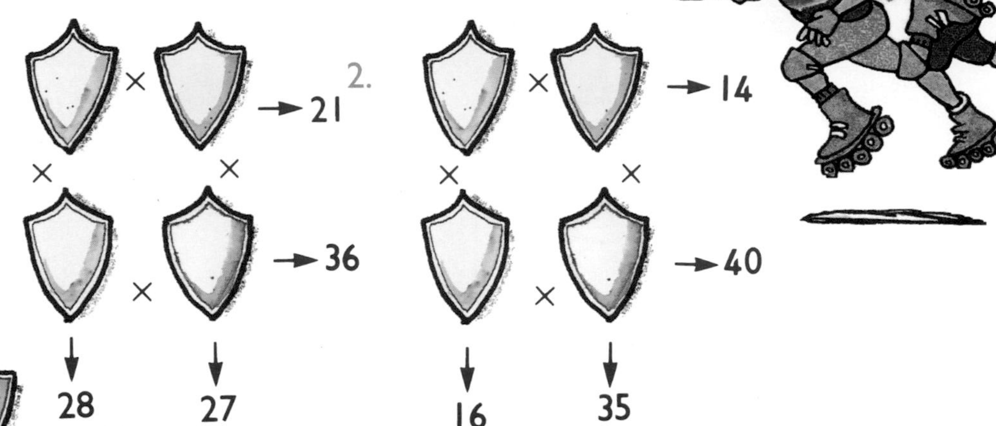
1.
× → 21
× ×
× → 36
28
27
2.
× → 14
× ×
× → 40
16
35

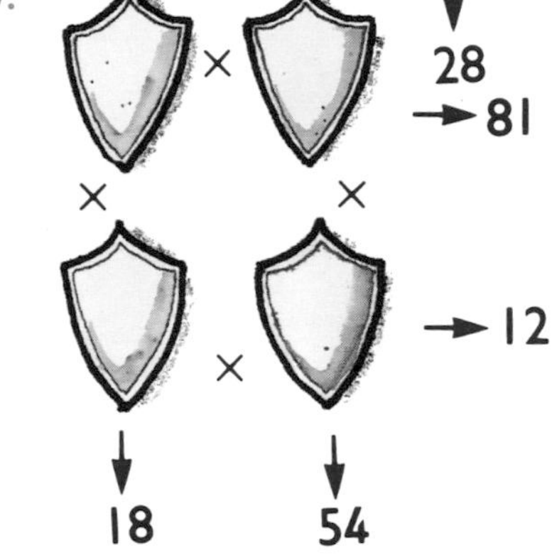
3.
× → 81
× ×
× → 12
18
54

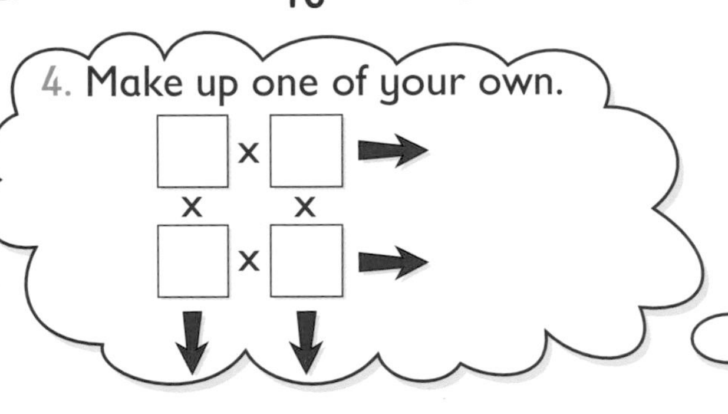
4. Make up one of your own.
×
× ×
×

B Copy and finish these patterns.

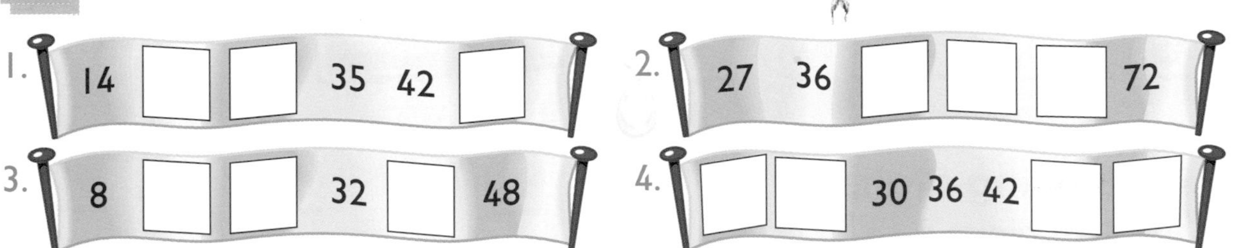
1. 14 35 42
2. 27 36 72
3. 8 32 48
4. 30 36 42

C Write which numbers went into each machine.

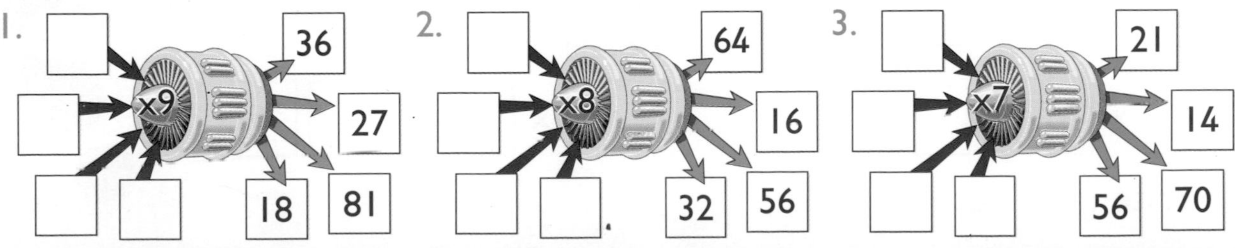
1. x9
36
27
18
81
2. x8
64
16
32
56
3. x7
21
14
56
70

Puzzle page

A The answers have been written in this puzzle.
Write the questions, which must be multiplication facts.

[1] 3	2	■	[2] 2	5	■
6	■	[3] 1	8	■	[4] 3
■	[5] 4	5	■	[6] 8	0
[7] 6	0	■	[8] 2	1	■
3	■	[9] 5	4	■	[10] 1
■	[11] 6	4	■	[12] 7	2

Across	Down
1. 8×4	1. 4×9
2.	2.
3.	3.
5.	4.
6.	5.
7.	6.
8.	7.
9.	8.
11.	9.
12.	10.

B Calculator target

Using only the highlighted keys find different ways to hit the target.

96
ON/C
OFF
8
4
5
6
×
2
3
=
TARGET 96

Here is one to start you off:

4 × 6 × 4 = 96

C Missing digits

Use digits 0 to 9

Find a place for each of these digits:

1 2 5 6 9 0 3 4 7 8

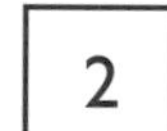

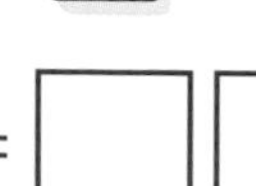

□ × □ = 2 4   □ □ × 7 = □ 0

□ × 8 = □ □   □ × □ = □ 5

Write your results.

D Multiple maze game

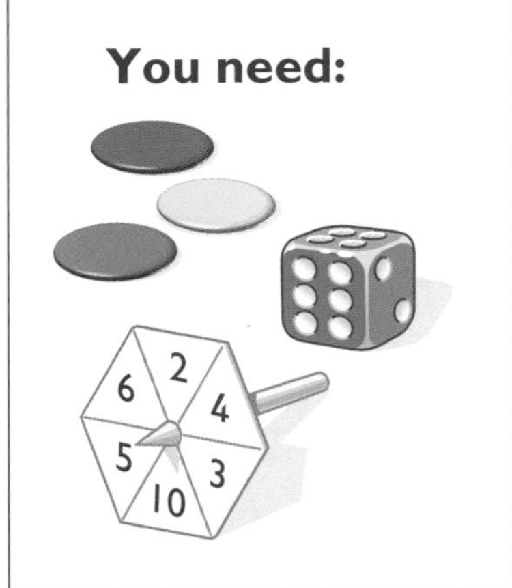

You need:
2
4
3
10
5
6

INFORMATION BOARD

Multiples of 3 3, 6, 9, 12, 15, 18...	Multiples of 4 4, 8, 12, 16, 20...
Multiples of 5 5, 10, 15, 20, 25...	Multiples of 6 6, 12, 18, 24, 30...

Rules:

1. Take turns to roll the dice or use the spinner.
2. Follow a path of multiples of the number thrown until you cannot go any further.
3. First to the finish is the winner.
4. You cannot move diagonally.

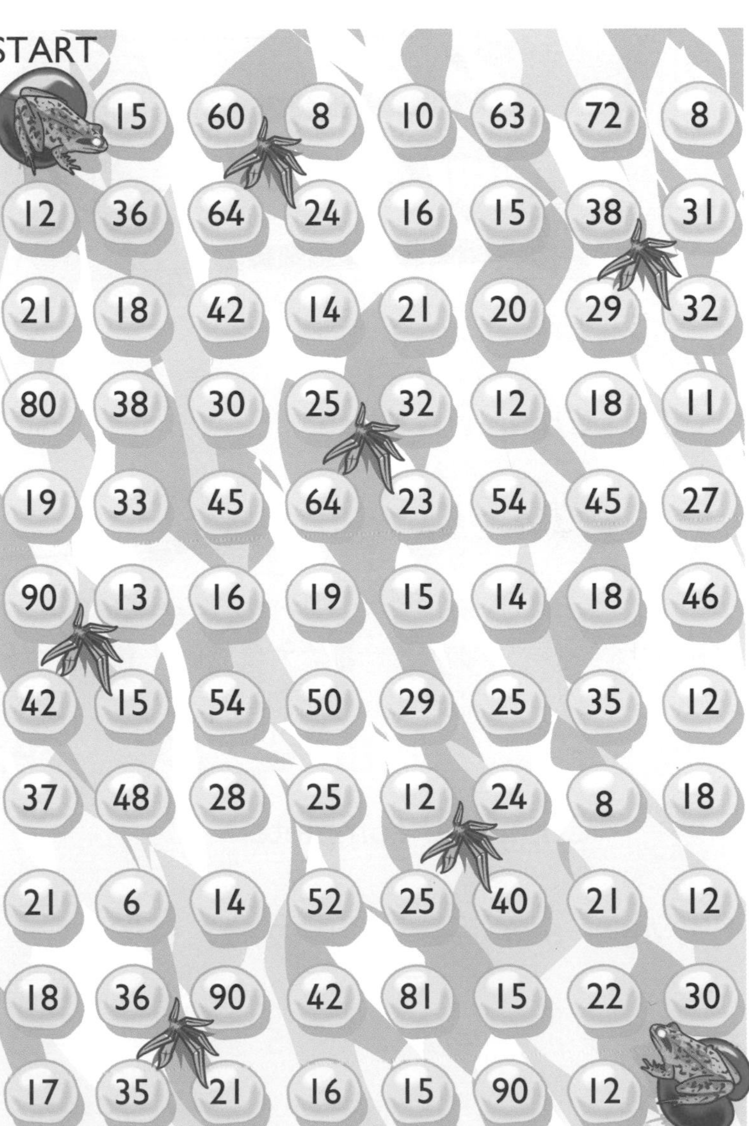

START
15 60 8 10 63 72 8
12 36 64 24 16 15 38 31
21 18 42 14 21 20 29 32
80 38 30 25 32 12 18 11
19 33 45 64 23 54 45 27
90 13 16 19 15 14 18 46
42 15 54 50 29 25 35 12
37 48 28 25 12 24 8 18
21 6 14 52 25 40 21 12
18 36 90 42 81 15 22 30
17 35 21 16 15 90 12
FINISH

Divide and multiply

A Write the numbers which entered the machine.

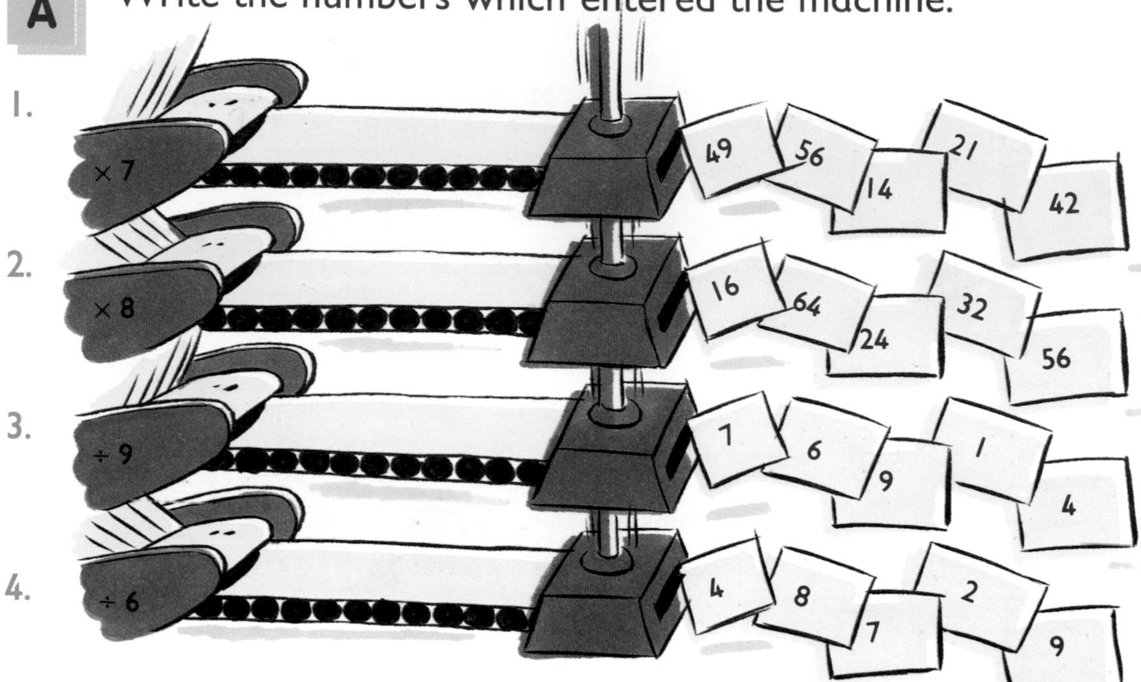
1.
× 7
49
56
14
21
42
2.
× 8
16
64
24
32
56
3.
÷ 9
7
6
9
1
4
4.
÷ 6
4
8
7
2
9

B Complete these.

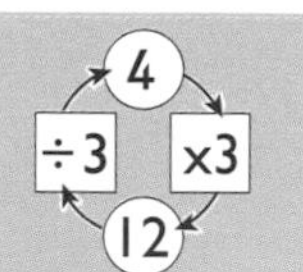
4
÷3
x3
12

1. 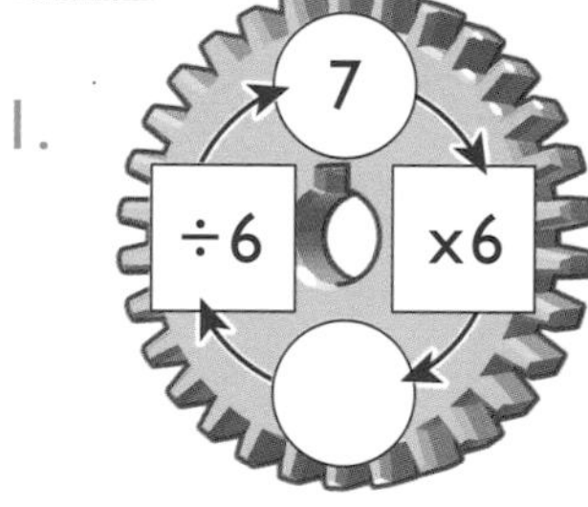
7
÷6
x6

2. 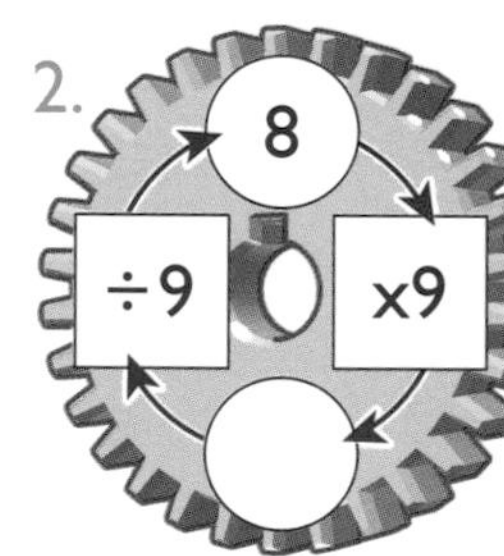
8
÷9
x9

3. 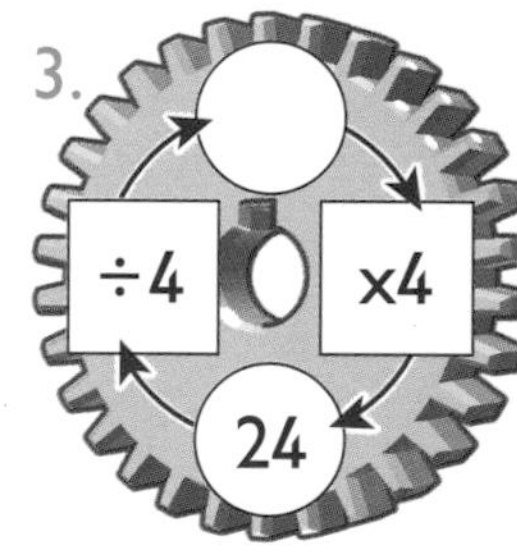
÷4
x4
24

4. 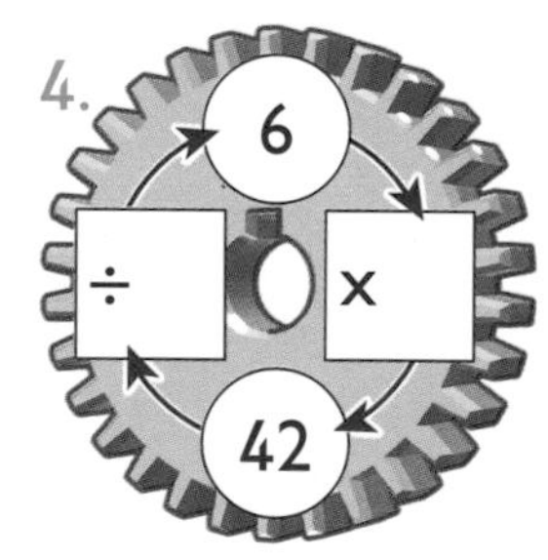
6
÷
x
42

C Copy and complete.

1. 48 ÷ 6 = ☐
2. 27 ÷ 9 = ☐
3. 56 ÷ 7 = ☐
4. 18 ÷ ☐ = 2
5. ☐ ÷ 7 = 3
6. 54 ÷ 9 = ☐
7. ☐ ÷ 8 = 8
8. 35 ÷ ☐ = 7
9. 28 ÷ 7 = ☐

Making a robot

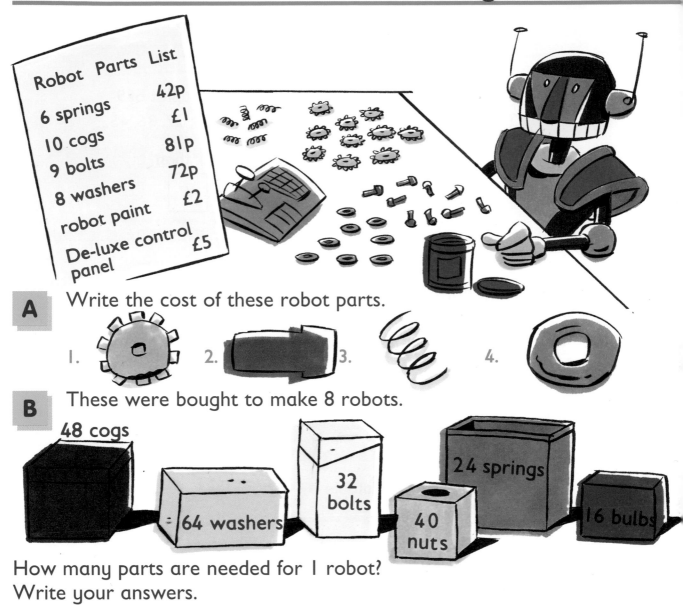

Robot Parts List

6 springs 42p
10 cogs £1
9 bolts 81p
8 washers 72p
robot paint £2
De-luxe control panel £5

A Write the cost of these robot parts.

1. 2. 3. 4.

B These were bought to make 8 robots.

48 cogs
64 washers
32 bolts
40 nuts
24 springs
16 bulbs

How many parts are needed for 1 robot?
Write your answers.

C Write the answers.

1. How many sixes in 42?
2. How many sevens in 56?
3. How many nines in 36?
4. How many fours in 28?

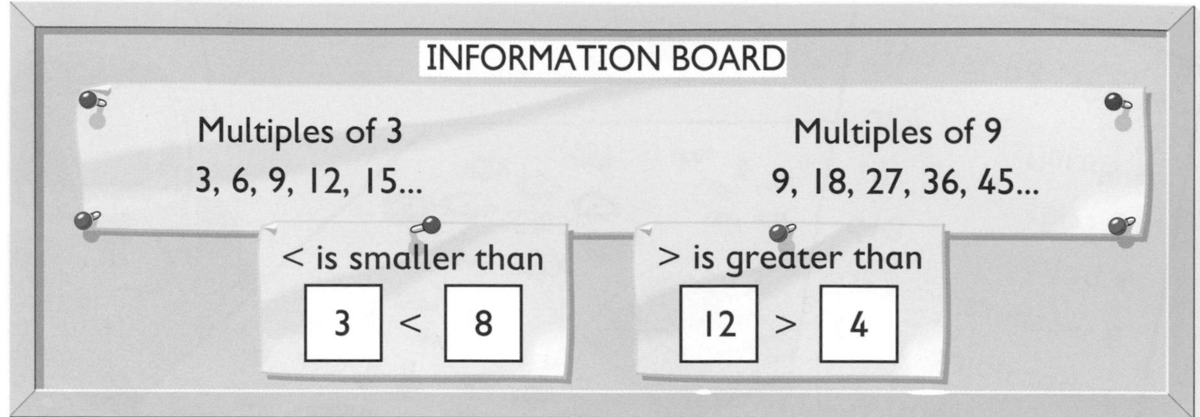
INFORMATION BOARD
Multiples of 3
3, 6, 9, 12, 15...
Multiples of 9
9, 18, 27, 36, 45...
< is smaller than
3 < 8
> is greater than
12 > 4

A Write the numbers 1 to 25 on small pieces of paper. Place numbers on this grid so that they follow the rules.

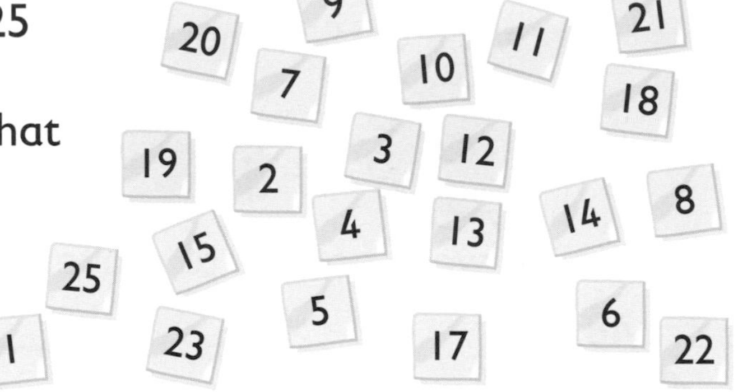
20
9
7
10
11
21
18
19
2
3
12
4
13
14
8
15
16
25
24
1
23
5
17
6
22

	Multiple of 5	Even number	Multiple of 3	>8
Odd number				
Multiple of 2				
<10				
Multiple of 4				

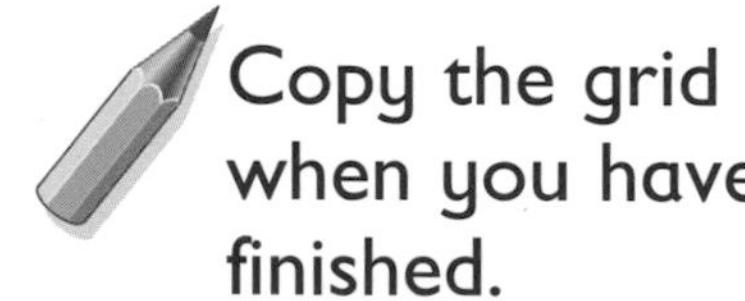
Copy the grid when you have finished.

B Copy these diagrams. Write the numbers 1 to 30 on each diagram.

1.

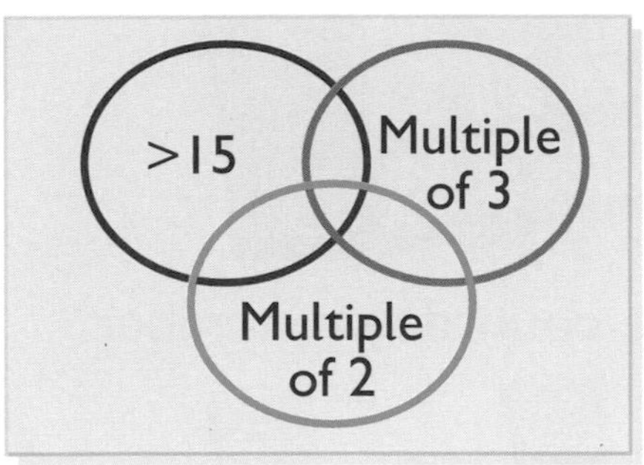

>15
Multiple of 3
Multiple of 2

2.

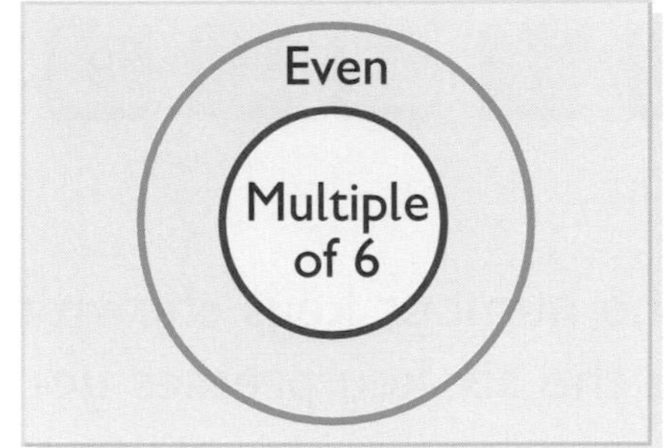

Even
Multiple of 6

3.

	Odd	Not odd
Multiple of 5		
Not a multiple of 5		

<15

C Follow each number through the sorting machine.

1. Copy and complete the table.

Container	Sorted numbers
A	
B	
C	
D	

2. Write five different numbers which would travel into container A.

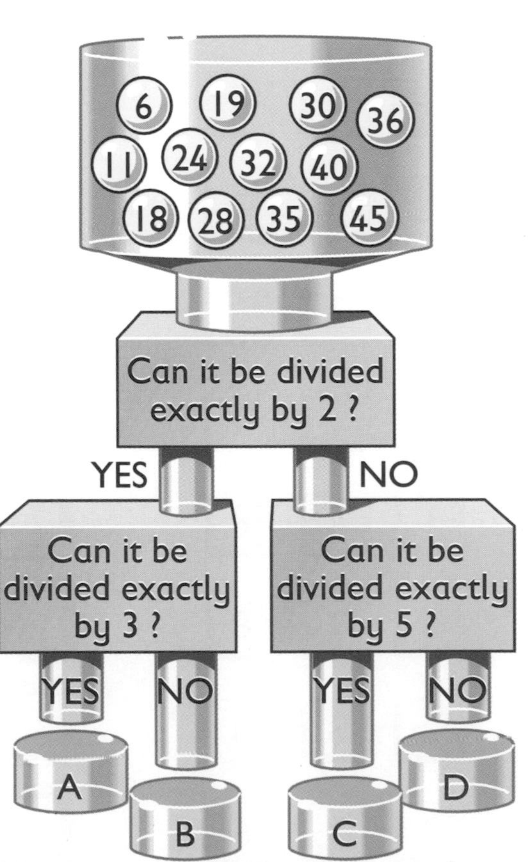

6
19
30
36
11
24
32
40
18
28
35
45
Can it be divided exactly by 2 ?
YES
NO
Can it be divided exactly by 3 ?
Can it be divided exactly by 5 ?
YES
NO
YES
NO
A
B
C
D

This is how 9, 8 and 3 can make 11.
Six key presses have been used.

11
ON/C
OFF
7 8 9 ÷
4 5 6 ×

Use the number keys shown to make the countdown number.
Write the six key presses you used.

1. 5 6 9 — 10
2. 3 5 6 — 9
3. 3 5 9 — 8
4. 3 4 5 — 7
5. 4 5 7 — 6
6. 1 3 9 — 5
7. 3 3 4 — 4
8. 1 4 8 — 3
9. 6 7 8 — 2
10. 2 3 8 — 1
11. 2 3 6 — 0

+
×
=
−
÷

Ancient maths

A Egyptian

The Egyptian numerals were:

I	∩					
1	10	100	1,000	10,000	100,000	1,000,000

Write what these numbers showed.

1.

2.

3.

B Greek

The Greek numerals were:

I	Δ	H	X	M	Γ	ΓΔ	ΓH	ΓX	ΓM
1	10	100	1,000	10,000	5	50	500	5,000	50,000

Write what these numbers showed.

1. HHHΔΔI
2. ΓH HHΔIII
3. ΓX XX ΓH ΓΔ ΔΓ

C Roman

The Roman numerals were:

I	V	X	L	C	D	M
1	5	10	50	100	500	1,000

Write what these numbers showed.

1. LXVII
2. CCLXXVII
3. MDCLV

Did You Know ?

Hypatia taught mathematics at Alexandria in Egypt. She was born in 370AD. She was one of the first woman scientists.

Multiplication

3 × 4 = 12

30 × 4 = 120

A

Copy and finish these.

1. 5 x 6 = ☐
   50 x 6 = ☐
2. 7 x 9 = ☐
   70 x 9 = ☐
3. 6 x 3 = ☐
   60 x 3 = ☐
4. 8 x 4 = ☐
   80 x 4 = ☐
5. 9 x 5 = ☐
   90 x 5 = ☐
6. 3 x 9 = ☐
   30 x 9 = ☐

B

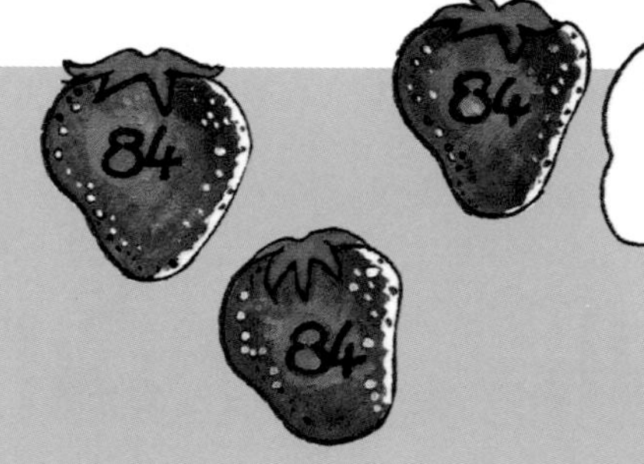
84
84
84

80x3 = 240
4x3 = 12
84x3 = 252

Multiply to find the totals.

1.

27
27
27
27

2.

56
56
56
56
56

3.

71
71
71

4.

19
19
19
19
19
19

5.

36
36
36
36

6.
98
98
98

C

Multiply units first then multiply the tens.
43
x 6
258

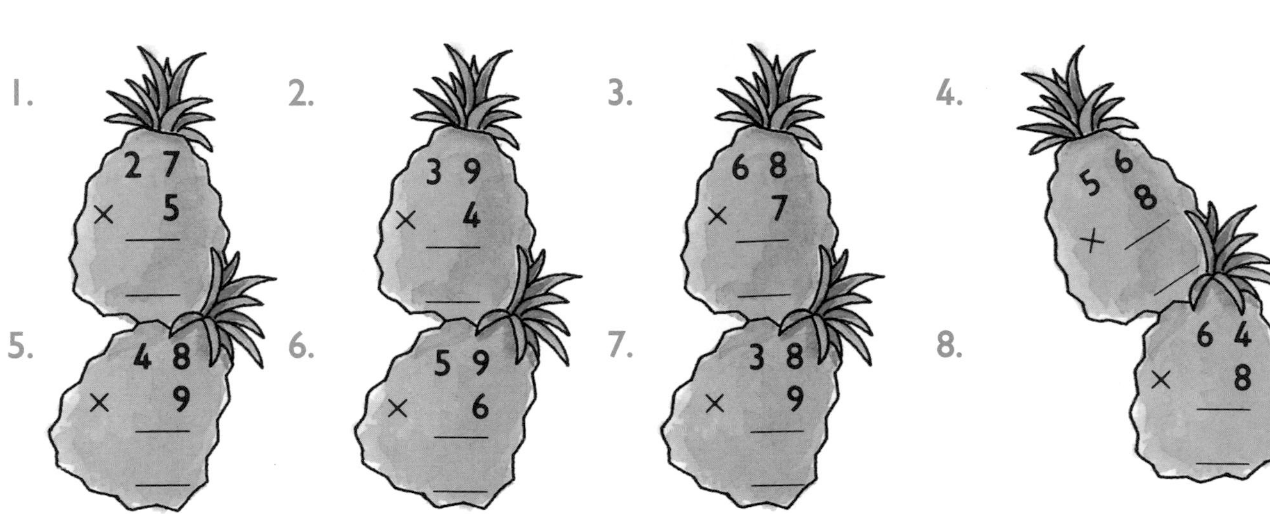
1.
27
× 5
2.
39
× 4
3.
68
× 7
4.
56
8
+
5.
48
× 9
6.
59
× 6
7.
38
× 9
8.
64
× 8

D

Write the cost of:

1. 7 oranges
2. 8 pears
3. 6 apples
4. 3 melons

FRUIT STALL

PRICE LIST	
1 orange	46p
1 pear	29p
1 apple	37p
1 melon	85p

E

1. Write the largest answer.

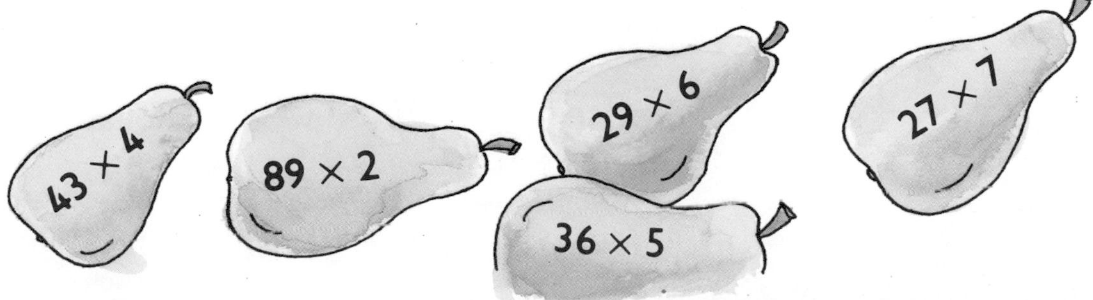
43 × 4
89 × 2
29 × 6
36 × 5
27 × 7

Summer camp

Write the sums to buy these.

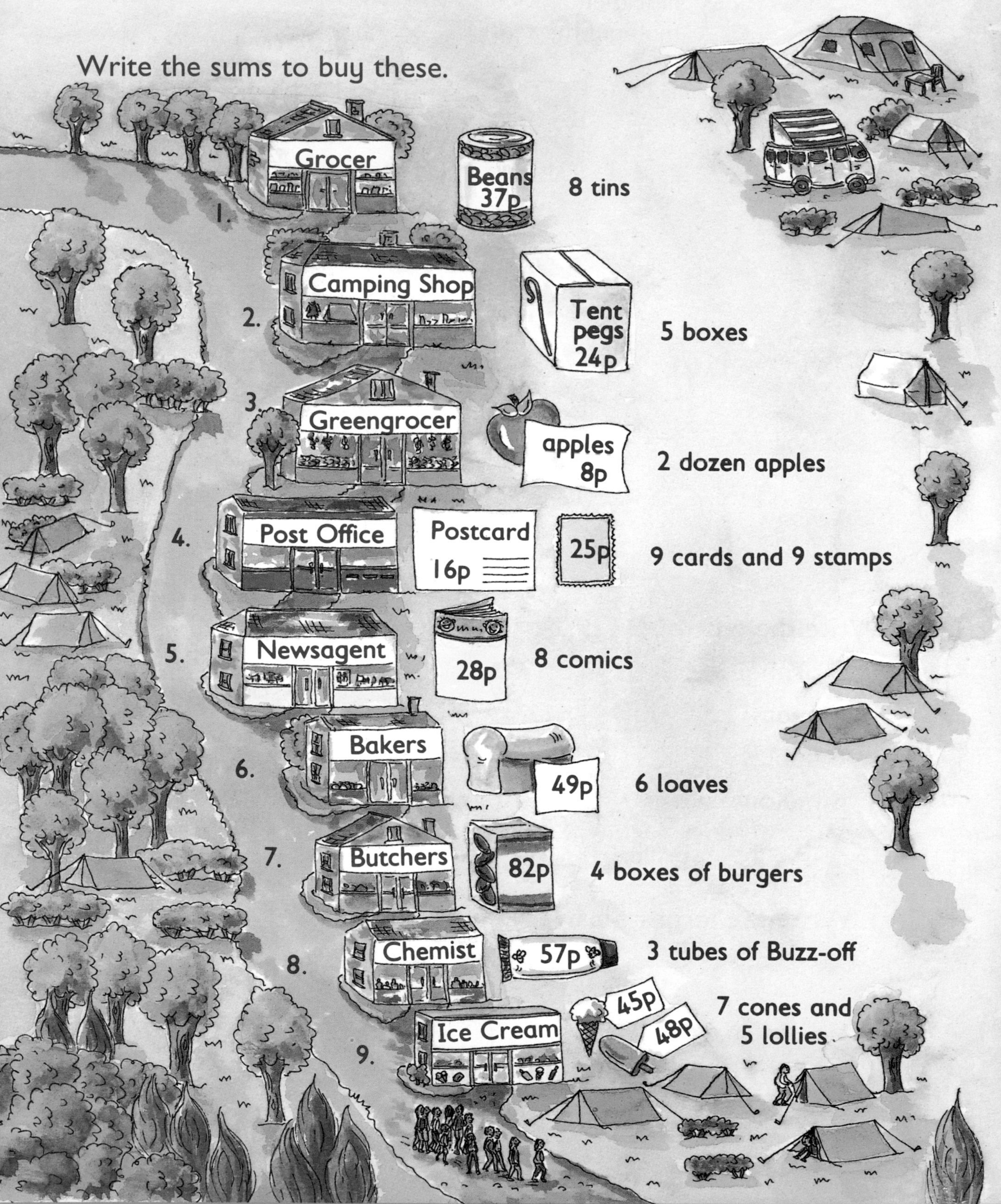
Grocer
Beans 37p
1.
8 tins
Camping Shop
Tent pegs 24p
2.
5 boxes
Greengrocer
apples 8p
3.
2 dozen apples
Post Office
Postcard 16p
25p
4.
9 cards and 9 stamps
Newsagent
28p
5.
8 comics
Bakers
49p
6.
6 loaves
Butchers
82p
7.
4 boxes of burgers
Chemist
57p
8.
3 tubes of Buzz-off
Ice Cream
45p
48p
9.
7 cones and 5 lollies

Finger multiplication

Russian multiplication

In the past Russian peasants used their fingers to multiply.
This is how they did it.

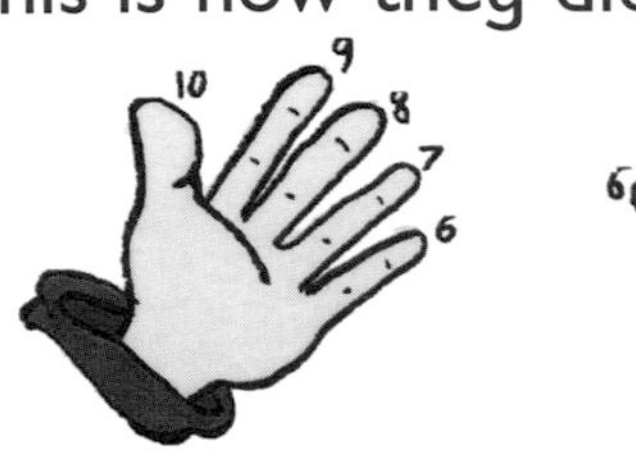
10
9
8
7
6

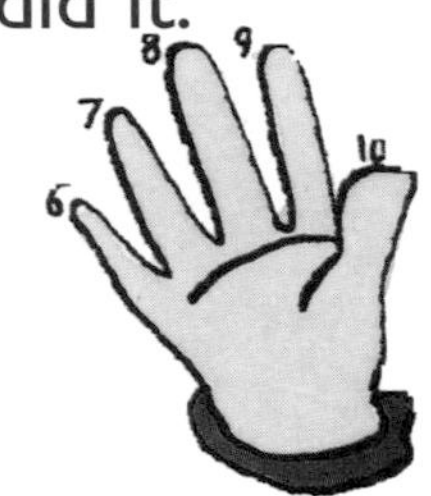
8
9
7
6
10

They numbered their fingers from 6 to 10.

To answer 8 × 7 they would touch the tip of an 8 finger to the tip of a 7 finger.

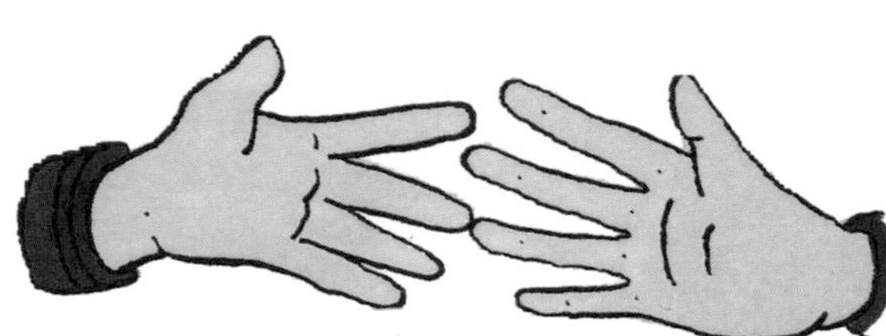

Touching fingers and those below give the tens number 50 .
The units number was found by multiplying remaining left hand and right hand fingers 2 × 3 .
So 8 × 7 = 56 .

Try this method for multiplying other numbers.

Finger nines

For many years fingers have been used to answer the 9× table.

Number your fingers.

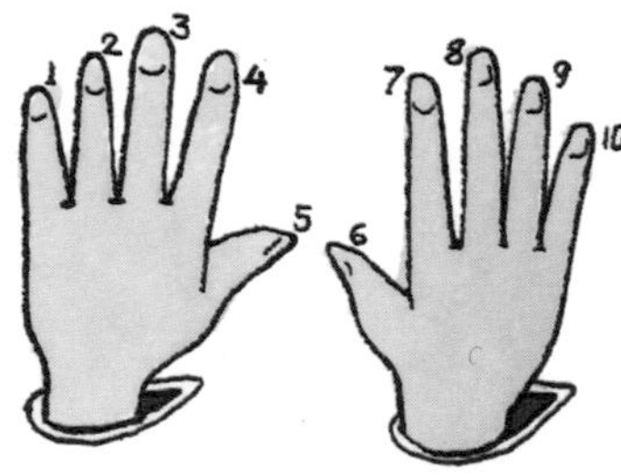
1
2
3
4
5

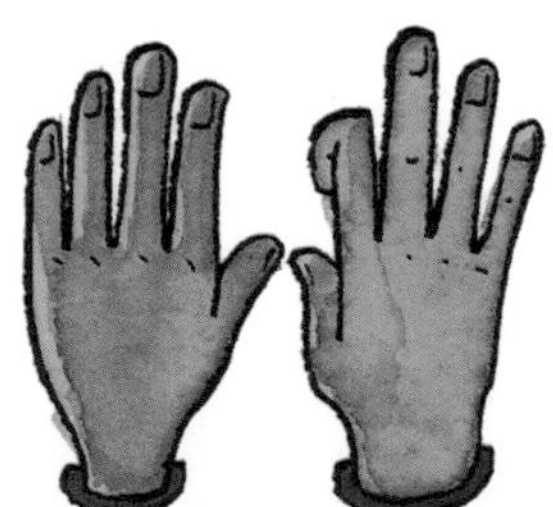
6
7
8
9
10

To answer 9 × 7 hold down the seventh finger. There are six fingers to the left and three fingers to the right.
So 9 × 7 = 63

Write which 9× table facts these show.

1.

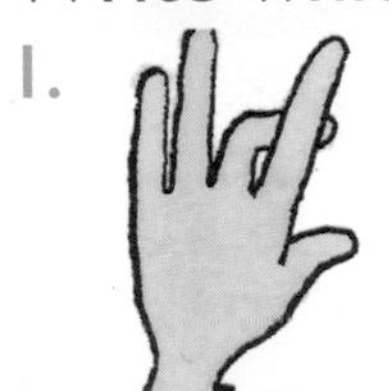

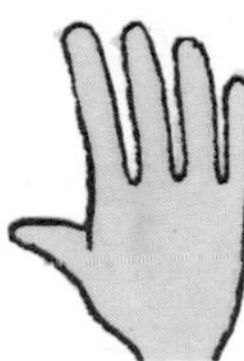

2.

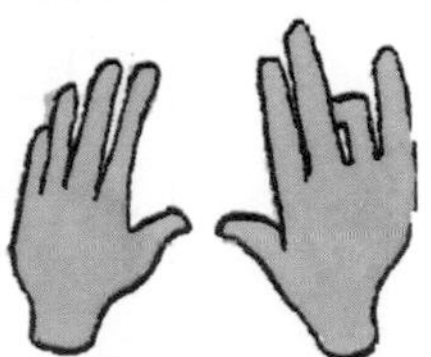

3.

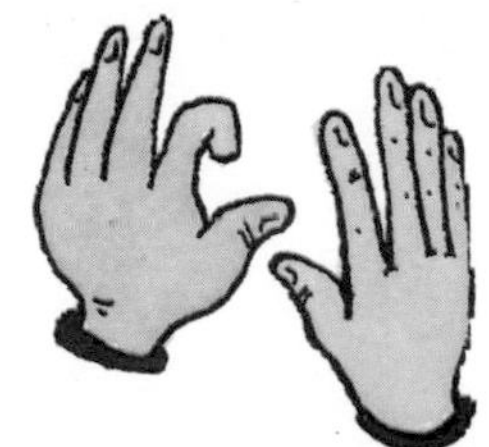

Try some of your own.

Number patterns

A Copy and write the answers.
Try to guess some without using a calculator.

3 × 9
3 × 99
3 × 999
3 × 9999
3 × 99999
3 × 999999
3 × 9999999

4 × 9
4 × 99
4 × 999
4 × 9999
4 × 99999
4 × 999999
4 × 9999999

5 × 9
5 × 99
5 × 999
5 × 9999
5 × 99999
5 × 999999
5 × 9999999

6 × 9
6 × 99
6 × 999
6 × 9999
6 × 99999
6 × 999999
6 × 9999999

7 × 9
7 × 99
7 × 999
7 × 9999
7 × 99999
7 × 999999
7 × 9999999

8 × 9
8 × 99
8 × 999
8 × 9999
8 x 99999
8 × 999999
8 × 9999999

B Write these numbers on small pieces of paper.

2

3

4

5

7

Arrange them on this multiplication sum.

x

Write the arrangement which gives you the largest answer.

Challenge

Choose five different digits of your own to make the biggest multiplication sum you can.

Fractions

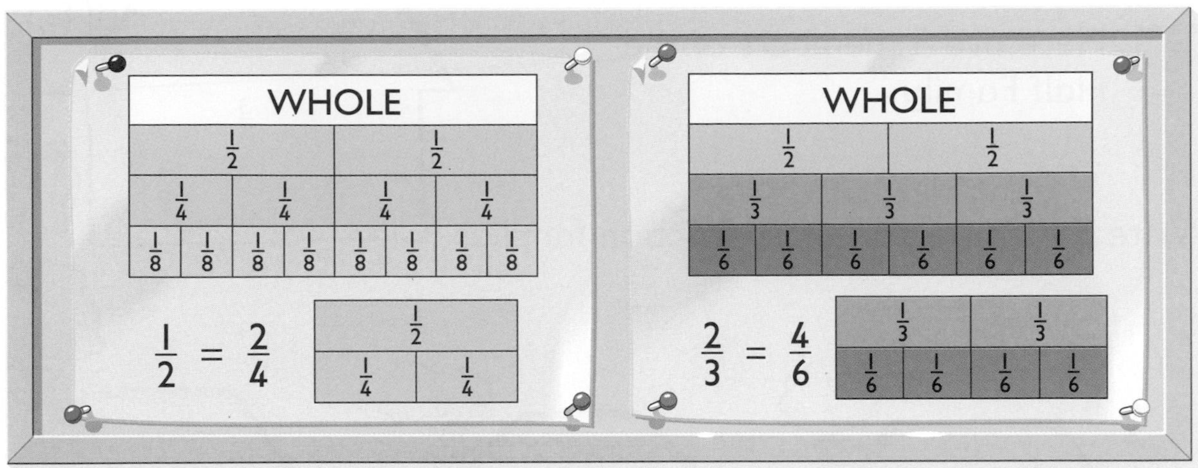
WHOLE
$\frac{1}{2}$ $\frac{1}{2}$
$\frac{1}{4}$ $\frac{1}{4}$ $\frac{1}{4}$ $\frac{1}{4}$
$\frac{1}{8}$ $\frac{1}{8}$ $\frac{1}{8}$ $\frac{1}{8}$ $\frac{1}{8}$ $\frac{1}{8}$ $\frac{1}{8}$ $\frac{1}{8}$
$\frac{1}{2} = \frac{2}{4}$
$\frac{1}{2}$
$\frac{1}{4}$ $\frac{1}{4}$
WHOLE
$\frac{1}{2}$ $\frac{1}{2}$
$\frac{1}{3}$ $\frac{1}{3}$ $\frac{1}{3}$
$\frac{1}{6}$ $\frac{1}{6}$ $\frac{1}{6}$ $\frac{1}{6}$ $\frac{1}{6}$ $\frac{1}{6}$
$\frac{2}{3} = \frac{4}{6}$
$\frac{1}{3}$ $\frac{1}{3}$
$\frac{1}{6}$ $\frac{1}{6}$ $\frac{1}{6}$ $\frac{1}{6}$

A Copy and finish these.

1. $\frac{1}{2} = \frac{\square}{8}$
2. $\frac{1}{2} = \frac{\square}{6}$
3. $\frac{1}{4} = \frac{\square}{8}$
4. $\frac{3}{4} = \frac{\square}{8}$
5. $\frac{1}{3} = \frac{\square}{6}$
6. $1 = \frac{\square}{8}$

B What fraction of each shape is red? Write each fraction in two ways.

$\frac{3}{12} = \frac{1}{4}$

1.

2.

3.

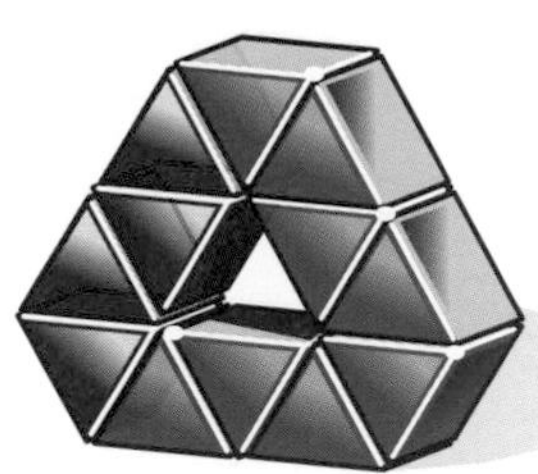

INVESTIGATE

Use 12 cubes to make a rectangle.
One-third of the cubes must be red.
Investigate different symmetrical patterns.

Fraction families

A Here are 5 members of the Half Family.

$\frac{1}{2}$

$\frac{6}{12}$ $\frac{2}{4}$ $\frac{3}{6}$ $\frac{5}{10}$ $\frac{4}{8}$

Write 5 members of these fraction families.

1.
$\frac{1}{4}$
2.
$\frac{3}{4}$
3.
$\frac{2}{3}$

B

INFORMATION BOARD
$\frac{1}{2} > \frac{3}{8}$
is greater than
$\frac{1}{6} < \frac{1}{3}$
is smaller than

Write the fractions.
Put > or < between each pair.

1.

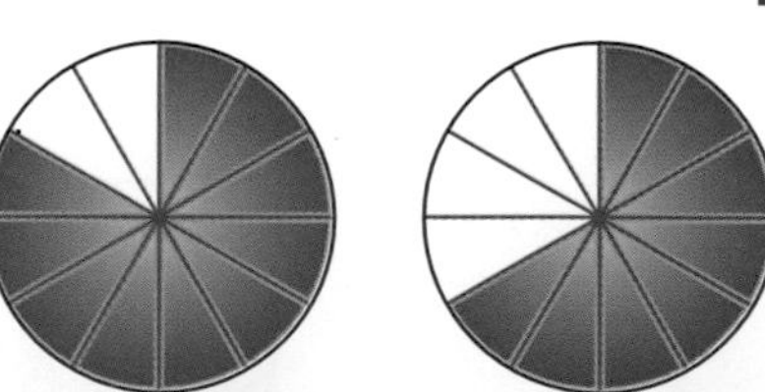

2.

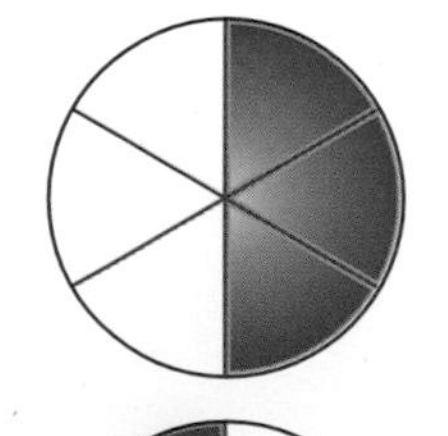

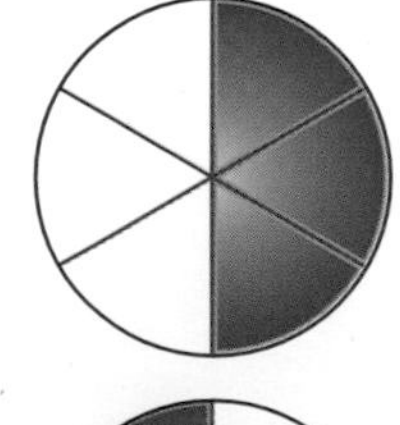

3.

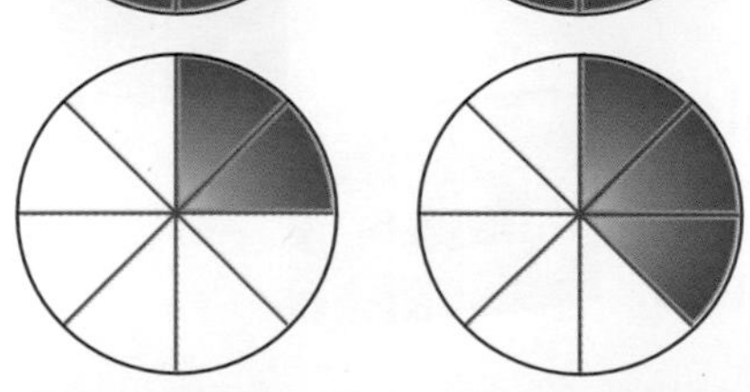

4.

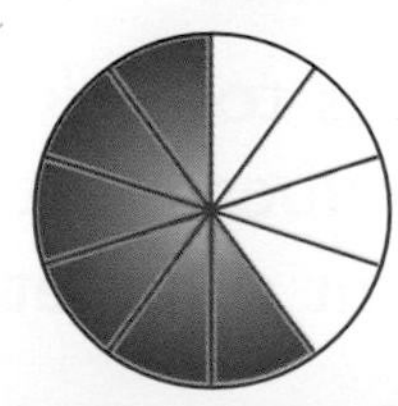

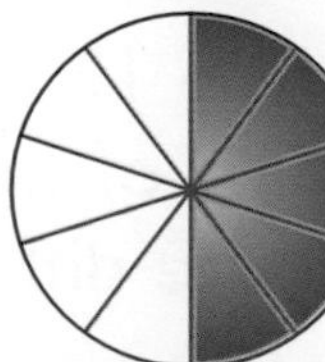

Tenths

A This shape is divided into tenths.

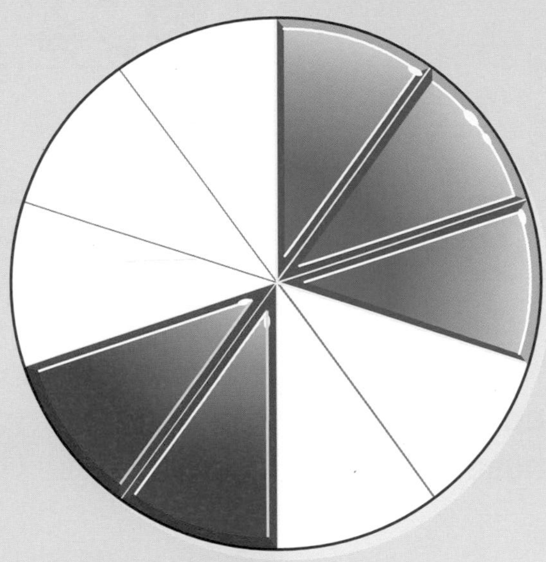

1. What fraction is coloured red?
2. What fraction is coloured blue?
3. What fraction is not coloured?

Write the fractions.

B Put in the missing numbers.

1. $1\frac{1}{2} = 1\frac{\square}{10}$
2. $\frac{1}{5} = \frac{\square}{10}$
3. $2\frac{3}{5} = 2\frac{\square}{10}$
4. $\frac{4}{5} = \frac{\square}{10}$
5. $1\frac{2}{5} = 1\frac{\square}{10}$
6. $1 = \frac{\square}{10}$

C This number line is marked in tenths.

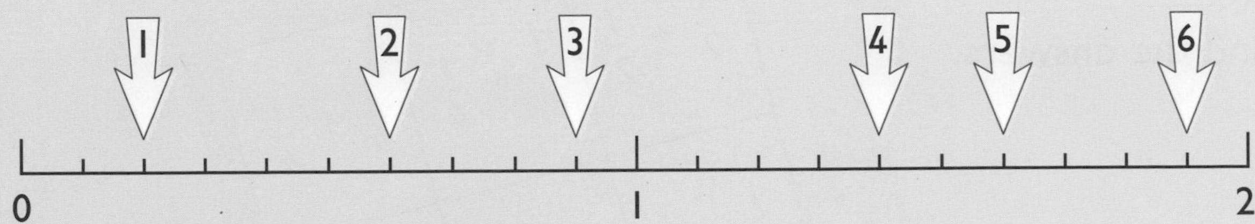
1
2
3
4
5
6
0
1
2

Write the fraction each arrow points to.

Sticker problems

Unit 4

A Stickers are sold in sheets like this.

$\frac{5}{12}$ of these stickers have been used.

$\frac{7}{12}$ have not been used.

Look at these sheets of stickers.
Write the fraction of stickers used.
Write the fractions of stickers unused.

1. 

2. 

3. 

4. 

5. 

6. 

Challenge

Find the answers.

1. $\frac{1}{2} + \frac{1}{2}$
2. $\frac{1}{2} + \frac{1}{4}$
3. $\frac{1}{4} + \frac{1}{4}$
4. $\frac{1}{2} - \frac{1}{4}$
5. $\frac{3}{4} - \frac{1}{2}$
6. $\frac{3}{4} - \frac{1}{4}$

Good guessing

49 × 3 is about
50 × 3, so the
answer is
approximately 150

A Write the approximate answer to these.

1. 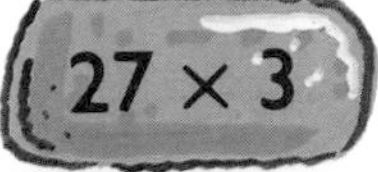
27 × 3

2. 
94 × 5
36 × 4

3. 
68 × 4
41 × 8

4. 99 × 6

5.

6.

B Write the approximate totals.

1. 
24 fish fingers
24 fish fingers
24 fish fingers
24 fish fingers

2. 18 hot dogs, 18 hot dogs, 18 hot dogs, 18 hot dogs, 18 hot dogs, 18 hot dogs, 18 hot dogs

3. 
Burgers
48 BURGERS
48 BURGERS
48 BURGERS
48 BURGERS
48 BURGERS
48 BURGERS

C 4, 5, 6 ... and 18, 19, 20 ... are consecutive numbers.

Write the consecutive numbers that make these answers.

1. ☐ × ☐ × ☐ = 504
2. ☐ × ☐ × ☐ = 720
3. ☐ × ☐ × ☐ = 120
4. ☐ × ☐ × ☐ = 24

Multiplying ants

A

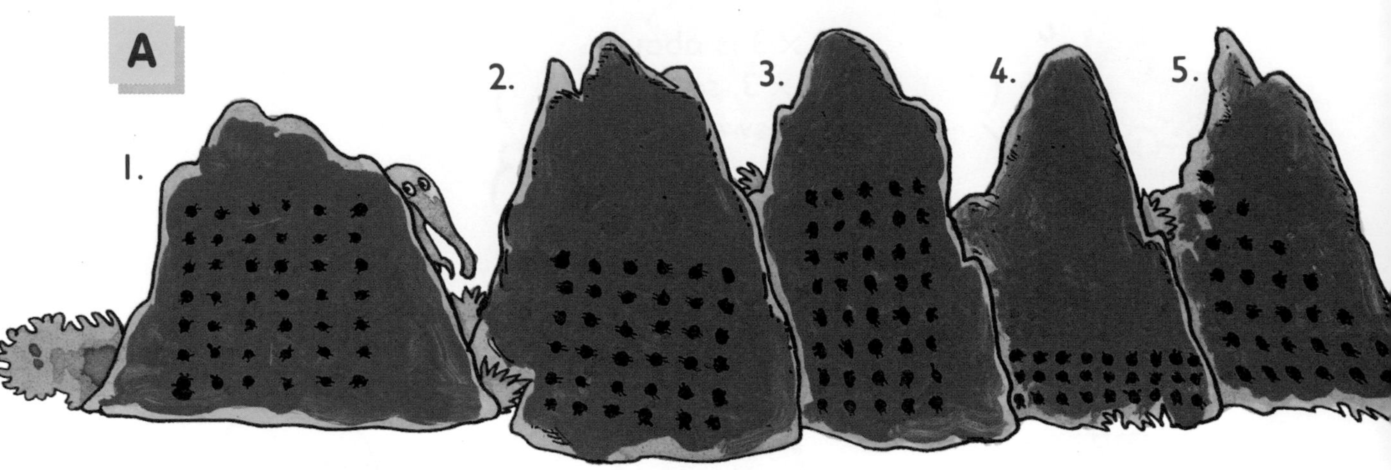
1.
2.
3.
4.
5.

Each year these ants multiply.
Copy and finish the ant multiplier chart.

	Number in anthill	×10	×100	×1000
1.				
2.				
3.				
4.				
5.				

B When full an ant hill holds 10 000 ants.
Estimate how many ants are in each anthill.

1. 3000, 300 or 30?
2. 7000, 700 or 70?
3. 3000, 900 or 90?

Unit 5 Estimating

A Write how far you think each boat has gone.

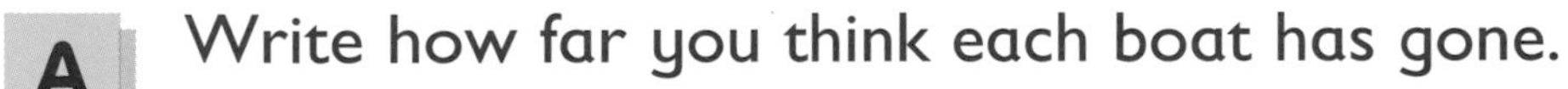

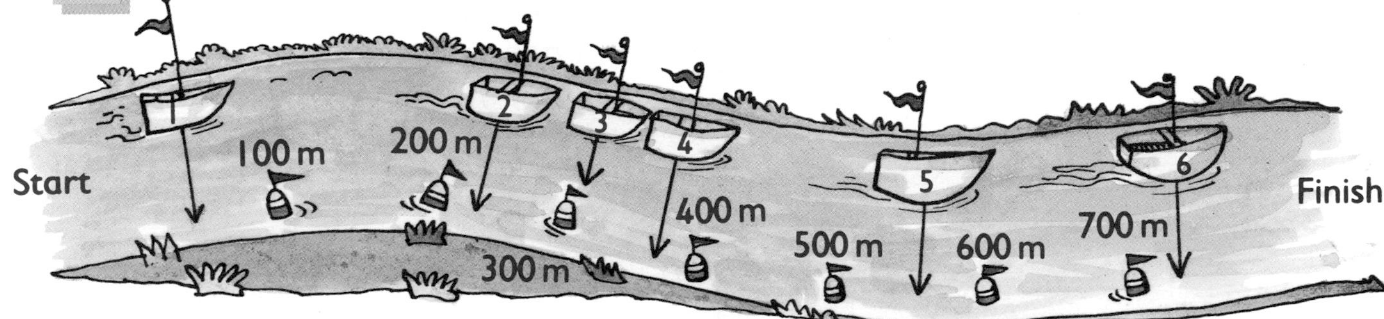

Start
1
2
3
4
5
6
100 m
200 m
300 m
400 m
500 m
600 m
700 m
Finish

B Write what you find at these positions.

1. 6550 m 2. 6120 m 3. 7090 m 4. 6370 m

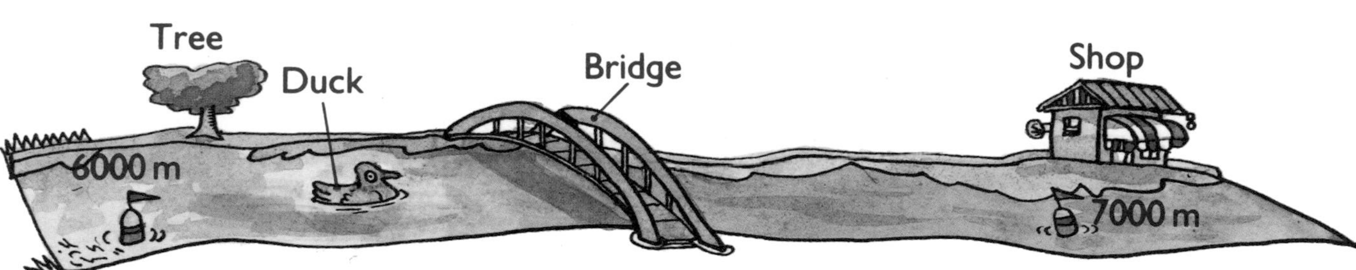

Tree
Duck
Bridge
Shop
6000 m
7000 m

C Write how deep you think each fish is swimming.

cm
100
200
300
1.
2.
3.
4.
5.
6.
7.

Square numbers

A Use squared paper.
Draw an increasing pattern of squares.
Write how many small squares are in each large square.

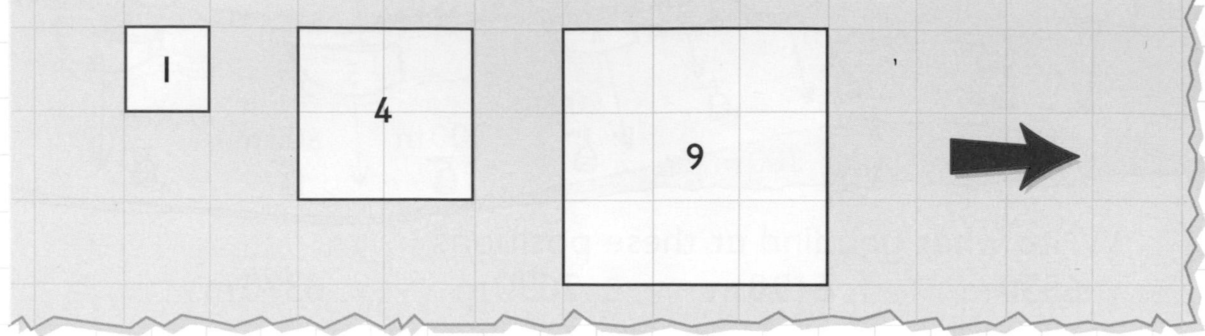
1
4
9

Write what you notice about the pattern.

B Use pegboard and pegs.
Make an increasing pattern of triangles like this.

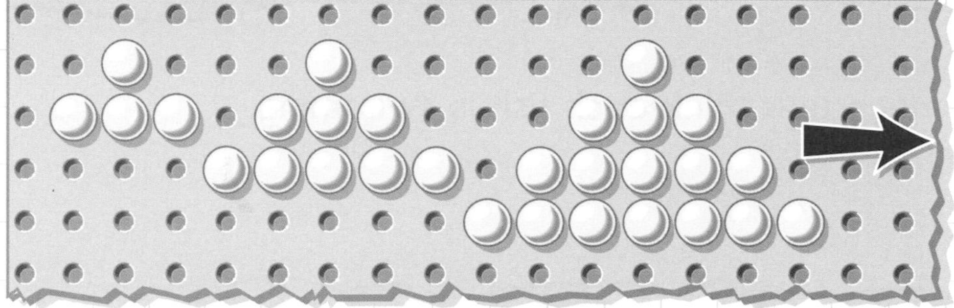

Write what you notice about the pattern.

C Use interlocking cubes.
Make an increasing pattern of L shapes like this.

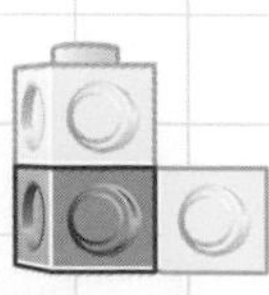

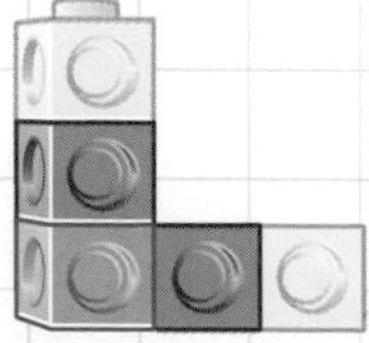

Fit the L shapes together to make squares.
Write what you notice about the pattern.

 Pegboard, pegs, cubes

D | 2×2, 3×3, 4×4, 5×5 … all make square numbers.

Write a list of all the square numbers to 100.

E Use a table square.

Colour in the square numbers. Write what you notice.

×	1	2	3	4	5	6	7	8	9	10
1	1	2	3	4	5	6	7	8	9	10
2	2	4	6	8	10	12	14	16	18	20
3	3	6	9	12	15	18	21	24	27	30
4	4	8	12	16	20	24	28	32	36	40
5	5	10	15	20	25	30	35	40	45	50
6	6	12	18	24	30	36	42	48	54	60
7	7	14	21	28	35	42	49	56	63	70
8	8	16	24	32	40	48	56	64	72	80
9	9	18	27	36	45	54	63	72	81	90
10	10	20	30	40	50	60	70	80	90	100

F Make a number spiral from 1 to 100 on squared paper.
Colour the square numbers.
Write what you notice.

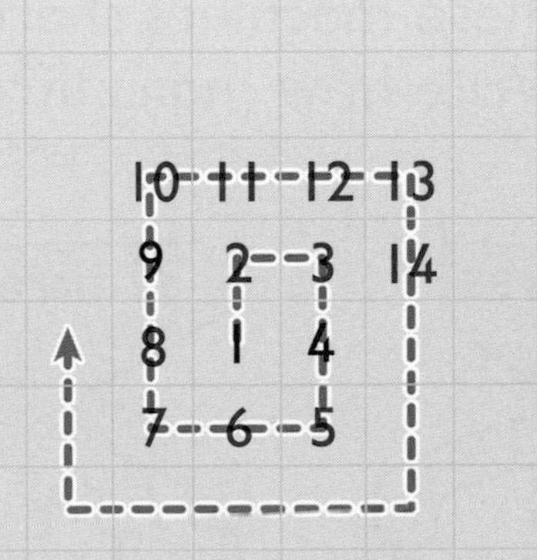
10 11 12 13
9 2 3 14
8 1 4
7 6 5

Dividing

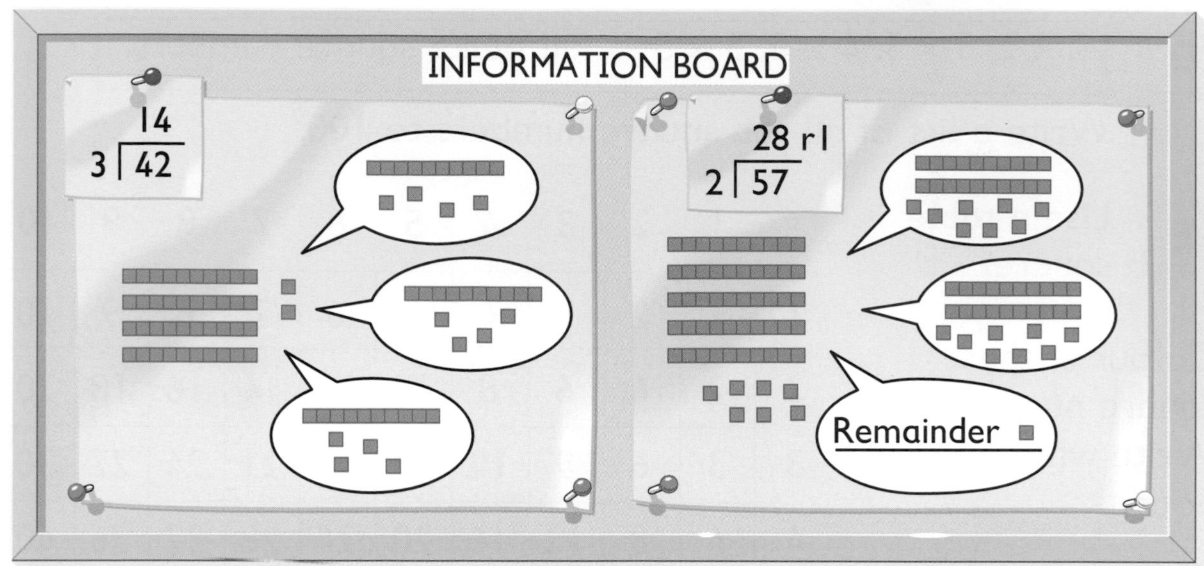
INFORMATION BOARD
14
3 | 42
28 r1
2 | 57
Remainder

A Use apparatus to do these.

1. $2\overline{)62}$
2. $3\overline{)84}$
3. $2\overline{)39}$
4. $4\overline{)92}$
5. $3\overline{)58}$
6. $4\overline{)75}$

B Now try these.

1. $3\overline{)78}$
2. $5\overline{)94}$
3. $4\overline{)64}$
4. $6\overline{)81}$
5. $4\overline{)49}$
6. $8\overline{)98}$

C These machines share equally.
Write how many litres in each bottle.

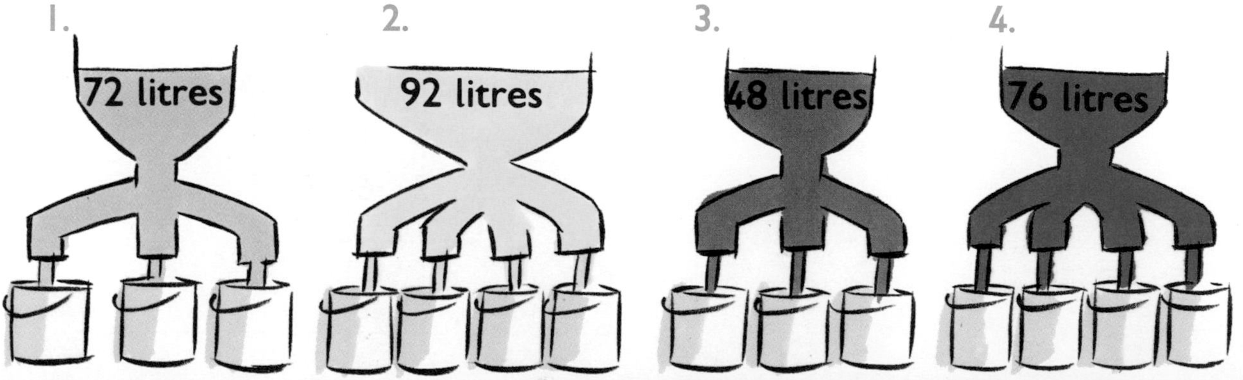
1.
72 litres
2.
92 litres
3.
48 litres
4.
76 litres

Unit 5 Rules for dividing

A All even numbers are divisible by 2.
Which of these numbers are divisible by 2?
Write your answers in order.

41
408
62
320
274
323
95
47
241
902

B Numbers which end in 0 are divisible by 10 and 5.
Numbers which end in 5 are divisible by 5.

85
73
125
340
915
875
392
335
900
490
605
505

1. Which of these numbers are divisible by 5? Write them in order.
2. Which of these numbers are divisible by 10? Write them in order.

C Leap year dates are divisible by 4. Write which of these events happened in a leap year.

Man on the Moon 1969
1948 Olympic Games London
1756 Mozart born
1558 Elizabeth 1 came to the throne

Challenge

Look at the last two digits of the numbers. Can you find a rule for testing whether a number is divisible by 4?

Fudge factory

A Write the answers to these.

1. How many in each box?

2. 72 sweets go into 3 boxes. How many in each box?

3. In the Tropical Fudge Box there are 84 sweets in 6 flavours. How many of each flavour?

4. In the Frosty Fruit fudge bag there are 95 sweets in 5 colours. How many of each colour?

5. How many sweets have nuts in them?

6. Naughty Norris ate $\frac{1}{3}$ of the Banana fudges. How many did he eat?

7. $\frac{1}{4}$ of the 48 sherbet surprises have been made. How many more are needed?

8. In the box of Mighty Mixture $\frac{1}{5}$ of them have wrappers. How many are unwrapped?

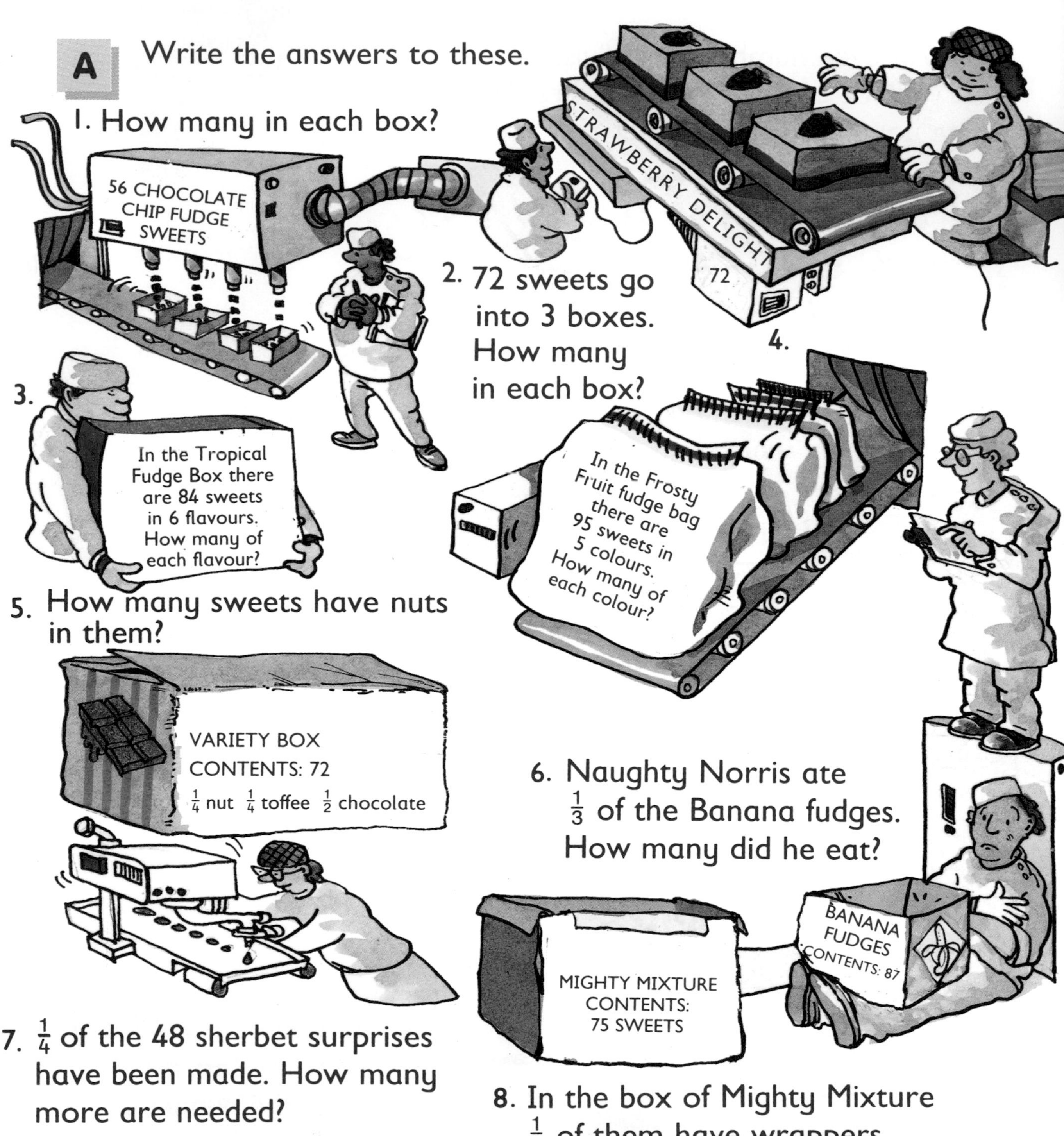

56 CHOCOLATE CHIP FUDGE SWEETS
STRAWBERRY DELIGHT
72
VARIETY BOX
CONTENTS: 72
$\frac{1}{4}$ nut $\frac{1}{4}$ toffee $\frac{1}{2}$ chocolate
BANANA FUDGES
CONTENTS: 87
MIGHTY MIXTURE
CONTENTS:
75 SWEETS

24p

19p
27p

63p

38p

52p

sticky toffee | banana | frost fruit | sherbert surprise | choc chip | strawberry delight

B Write the cost of each box.

1.

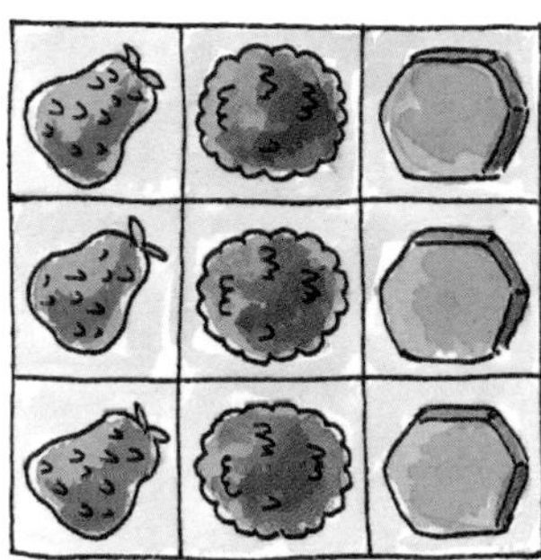

2.

3.

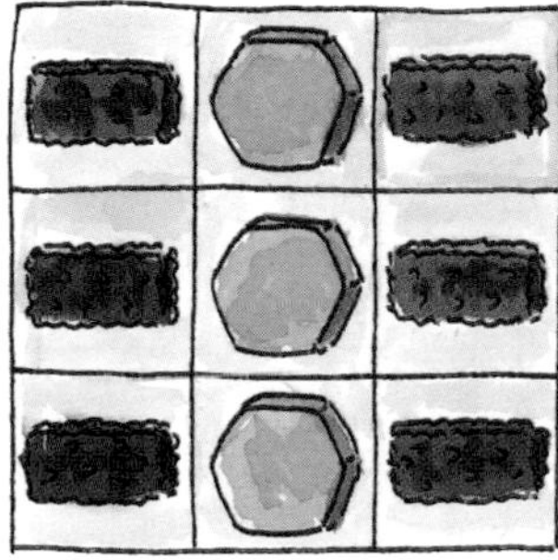

C

1. How many choc chip fudges can be bought for £2?
2. How many sherbet surprise fudges can bought for £5?
3. How many frosty fruit fudges can be bought for £2?
4. You have £5 to spend. Draw a chocolate box to show your selection. Write the price list.

D

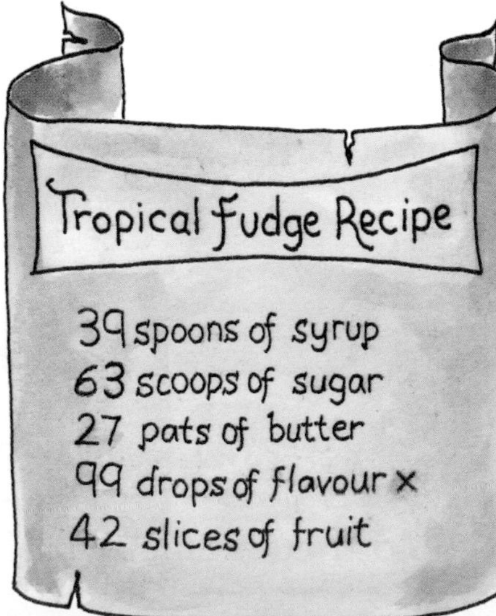
Tropical Fudge Recipe
39 spoons of syrup
63 scoops of sugar
27 pats of butter
99 drops of flavour x
42 slices of fruit

This recipe makes 18 boxes of Tropical Fudge.
Write the recipe to make 6 boxes of Tropical fudge.

Factors

Unit 6

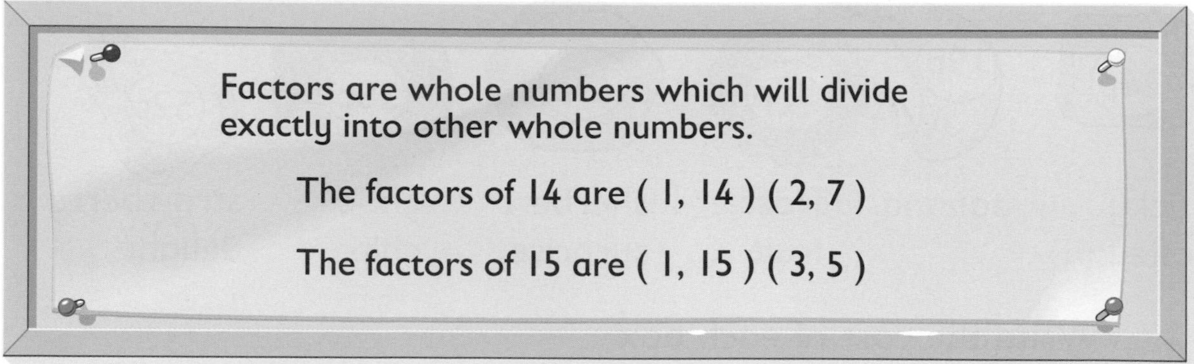

Factors are whole numbers which will divide exactly into other whole numbers.
The factors of 14 are (1, 14) (2, 7)
The factors of 15 are (1, 15) (3, 5)

A Write the factors of these numbers:

1. 12
2. 16
3. 

18

4. 

24

5. 

21

B Numbers can be changed into factors.

$18 = 2 \times 9$
$18 = 2 \times 3 \times 3$
$18 = 3 \times 6$

$16 = 4 \times 4$
$16 = 2 \times 2 \times 4$
$16 = 2 \times 8$
$16 = 2 \times 2 \times 2 \times 2$

Change these numbers into factors.

1. 30
2. 

12

3. 

24

4. 

20

5. 

32

Challenge

Here are some factors:

4
2
3

Which numbers, less than 50, could they be factors of?

Division star

A game for two or three players.
Roll two dice and total the numbers.
Cover any number on the star which this total will divide into exactly.
Choose which game to play.

Game 1
First to place 10 counters wins

Game 2
First to have 4 touching counters wins

35

16 9 24

70 15 8 54 2 7 50 48 72 100 42

11 90 88 80 77 60 66 18 27

45 49 22 44 12 14 55 81 6

63 20 36 21 25 33 5 4 24 10 56

40 28 30

32

Game 3
First to complete a star point wins

Game 4
The player who places most counters wins

Decimal numbers

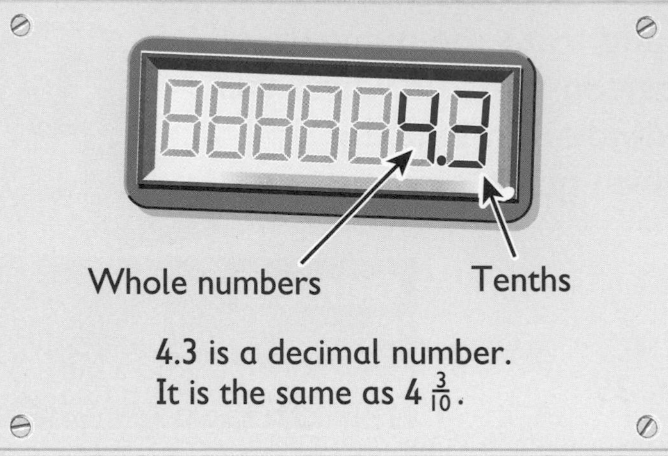
4.3
Whole numbers
Tenths

4.3 is a decimal number.
It is the same as $4\frac{3}{10}$.

A Write these decimals as fractions.

1. 
3.9

2. 
1.5

3. 
2.3

4. 
3.8

5. 
4.1

6. 
6.2

B Write these fractions as decimals.

1.  $2\frac{7}{10}$

2.  $1\frac{1}{10}$

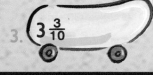

3.  $3\frac{3}{10}$

4.  $2\frac{9}{10}$

Challenge

Change these fractions to tenths and write them as decimals.

1. $1\frac{1}{2}$ 2. $4\frac{1}{5}$ 3. $2\frac{2}{5}$ 4. $1\frac{2}{5}$ 5. $3\frac{4}{5}$

Unit 6 Decimals

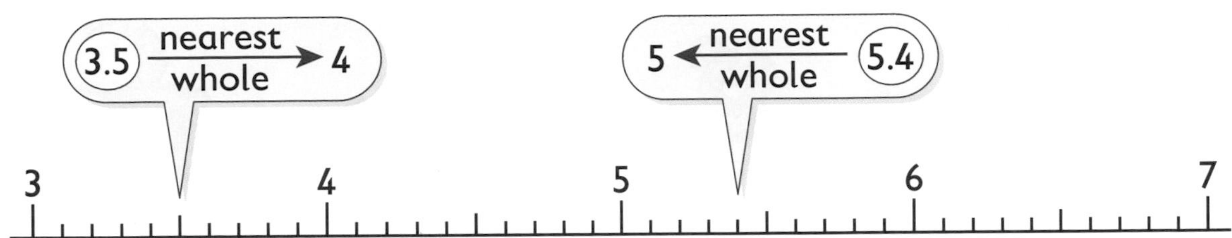

3.5 nearest whole 4
5 nearest whole 5.4
3
4
5
6
7

A Find these decimals on the number line.
Write the nearest whole number.

1. 3·8
2. 4·3
3. 6·2
4. 3·3
5. 5·9
6. 6·7

B Write these numbers on pieces of paper: 4 5 6

Choose pairs and put them in these boxes to make decimals.

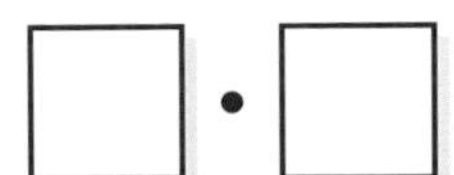

Write different decimal numbers and their nearest whole number.

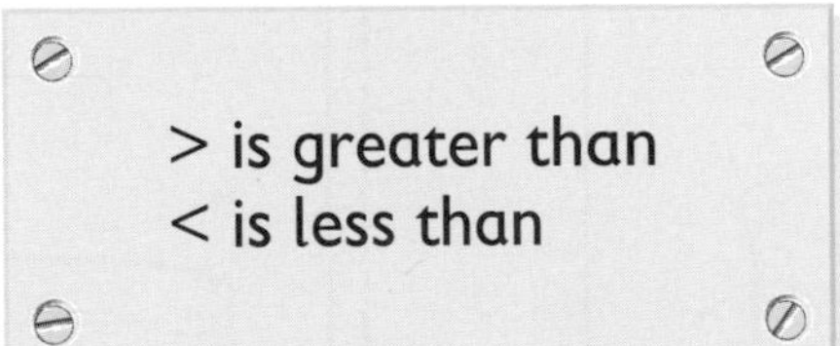

> is greater than
< is less than

Copy and write > or < between these numbers.
Use the number line to help.

1. $3\frac{1}{2}$ ☐ 3.3
2. $4\frac{1}{2}$ ☐ 4.6
3. $6\frac{1}{2}$ ☐ 6.4
4. $5\frac{1}{2}$ ☐ 5.7
5. $3\frac{1}{2}$ ☐ 3.2
6. $5\frac{1}{2}$ ☐ 5.8

Reading scales

A Write the weight of each dog.

1.

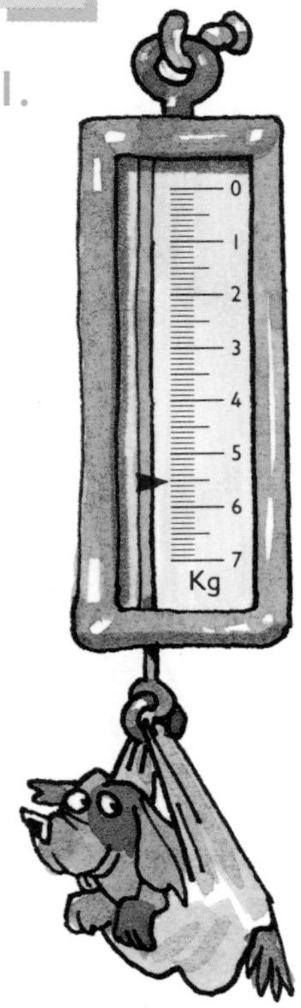

2.

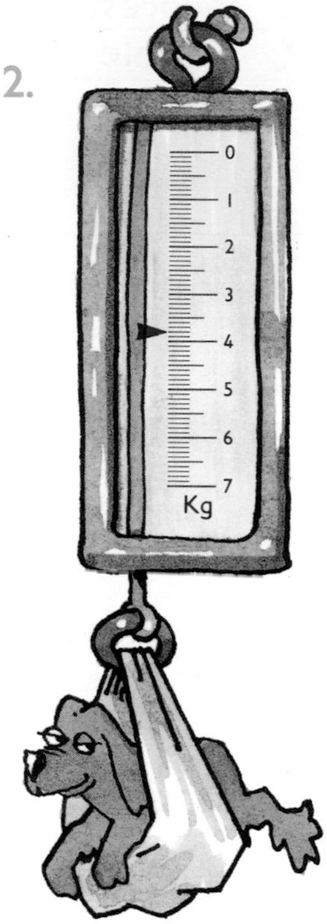

3.

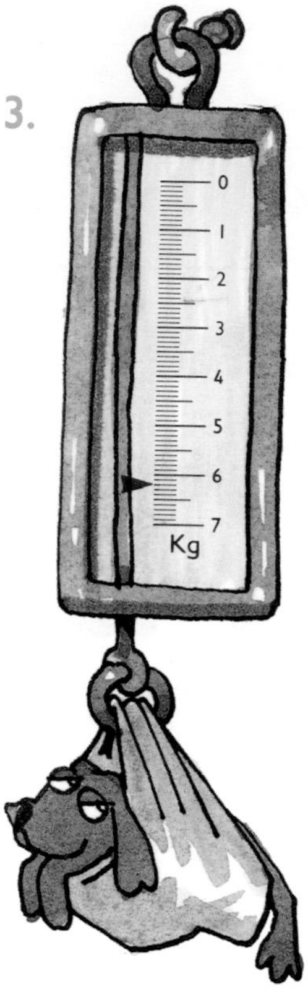

4.

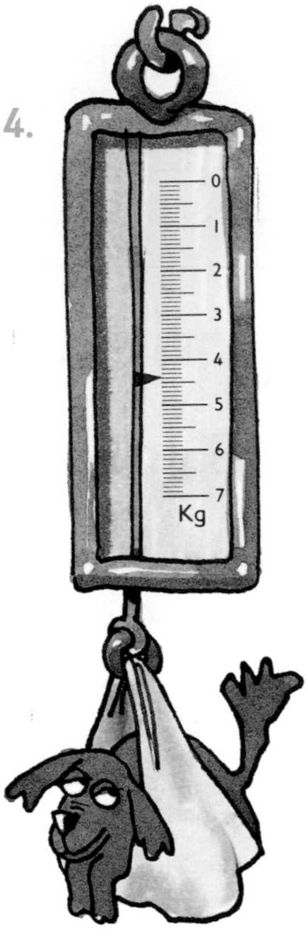

B Write how much water is in each jug.

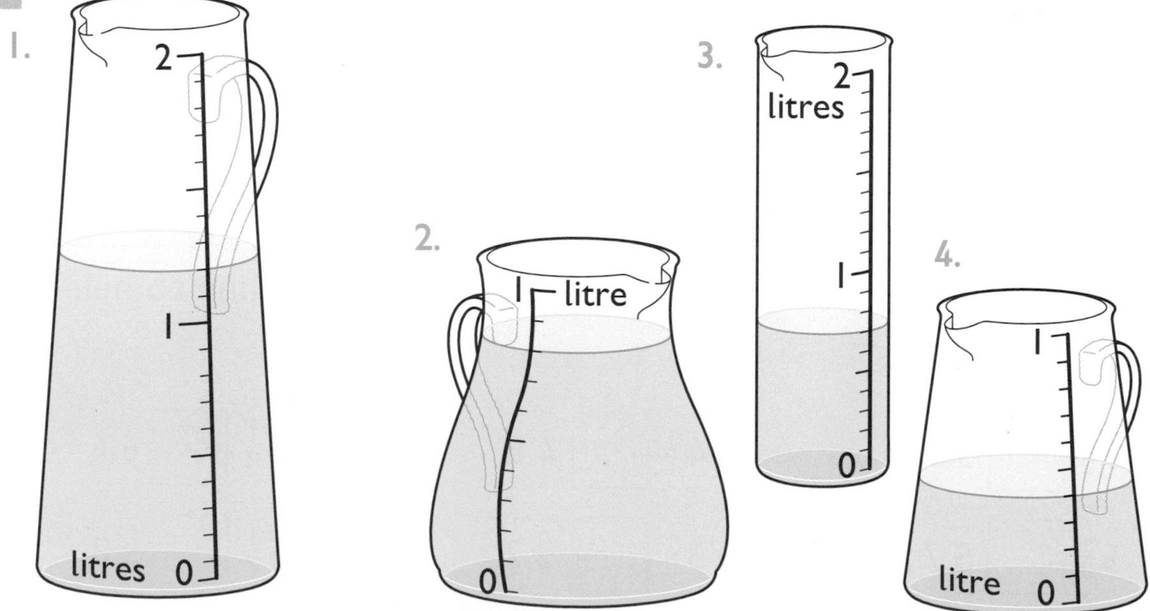
1.
2
1
litres 0
2.
1 litre
0
3.
2
litres
1
0
4.
1
litre 0

C Write the length of each bone.

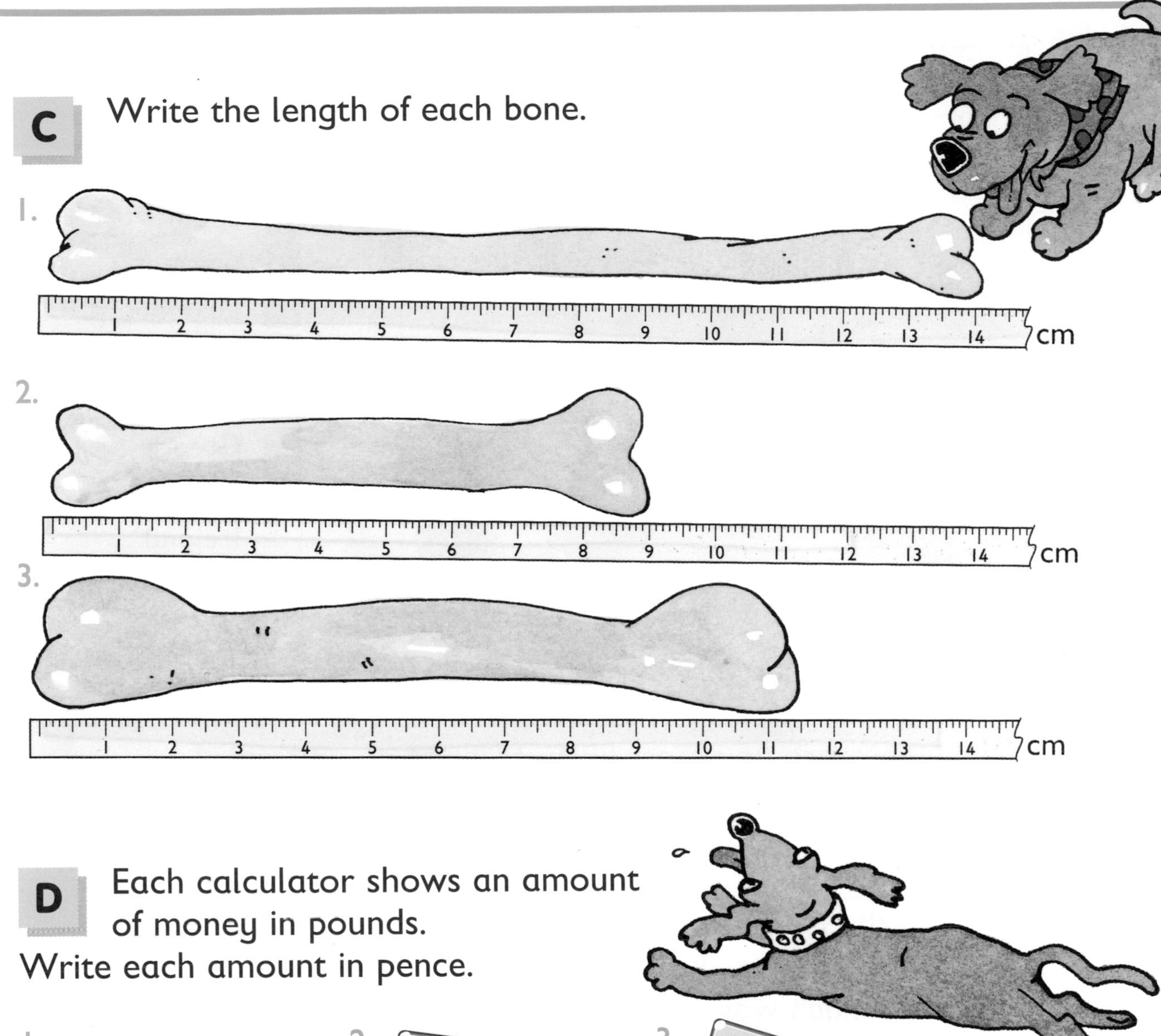

1\.

2\.

3\.

D Each calculator shows an amount of money in pounds.
Write each amount in pence.

1\. 2.6

2\. 3.4

3\. 1.8

Europe

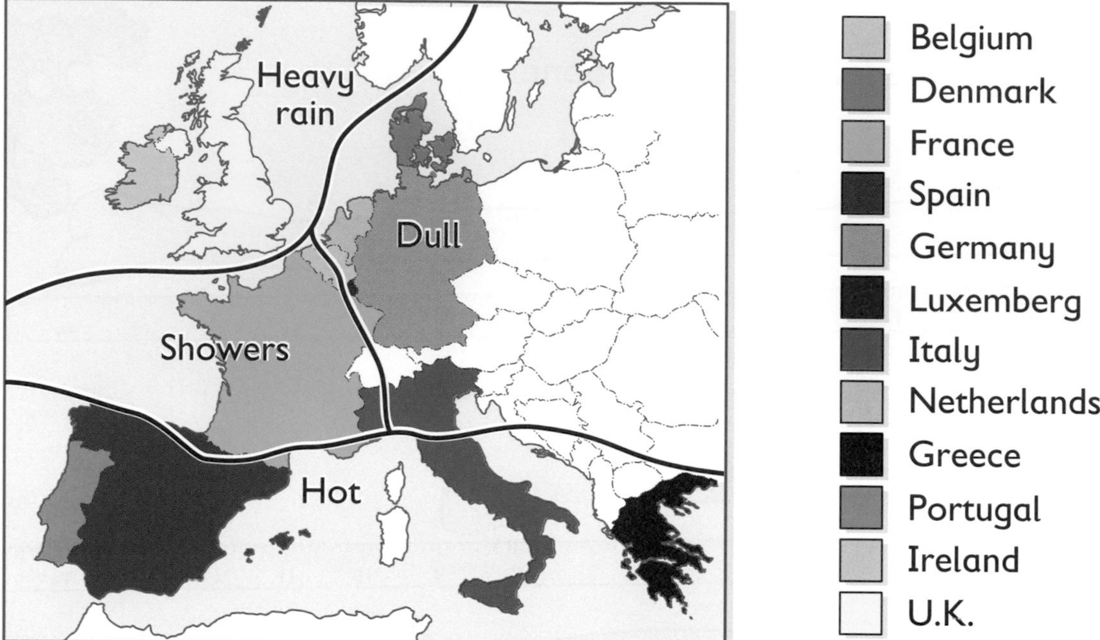
Heavy rain
Dull
Showers
Hot
Belgium
Denmark
France
Spain
Germany
Luxemberg
Italy
Netherlands
Greece
Portugal
Ireland
U.K.

A Write your answers in sentences.

1. Is it likely to rain in Spain?
2. Where are you most likely to need an umbrella?
3. What will the weather be like in Greece?
4. Will Portugal be brighter than Denmark?

B

1. Which city was coolest?
2. Which city was hottest?
3. How much warmer was Madrid than Brussels?
4. How much cooler was Paris than Athens?

City	Temp °C	City	Temp °C
Amsterdam	25	Lisbon	33
Athens	33	Luxembourg	25
Berlin	25	Madrid	34
Brussels	24	Paris	25
Copenhagen	20	Rome	32
Dublin	22	London	21

Challenge

Can you match each city to a country?

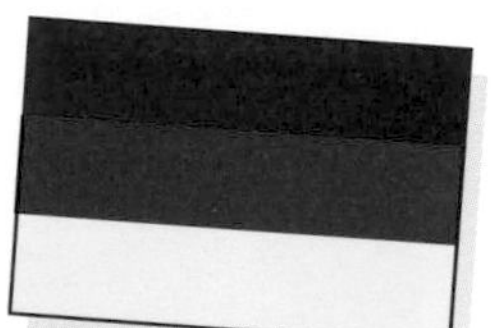

Country	Approx Area (km^2)	Approx Population
Belgium	31 000	9 880 000
Denmark	43 000	5 135 000
France	544 000	56 100 000
Germany	357 000	77 800 000
Greece	132 000	10 100 000
Ireland	70 000	3 515 000
Italy	301 000	57 200 000
Luxembourg	2 600	380 000
Netherlands	42 000	14 860 000
Portugal	92 000	10 370 000
Spain	505 000	39 150 000
UK	244 000	57 065 000

C Write your answers in sentences.

1. Which country has the largest area?
2. Which three countries have a population of about 10 million?
3. Which country is about $\frac{1}{3}$ the size of Portugal?

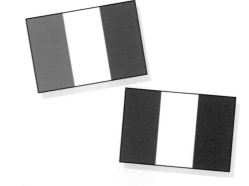

Challenge

Which country is the most crowded?
Write how you worked it out.

A Write these temperatures:

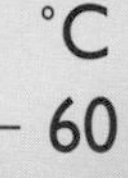

1. A very hot temperature recorded at Al'Aziziyah in Libya.

2. This temperature has been recorded in Death Valley, California.

3. Australia gets hot; this temperature was recorded at Cloncurry, Queensland.

4. Europe can become very hot. This temperature was recorded at Cordoba in Spain.

°C: 60, 50, 40, 30, 20, 10, 0, -10, -20, -30, -40, -50, -60, -70, -80, -90

5. Europe can be very cold. This was recorded at Sodankyla in Finland.

6. Canada is sometimes very cold. This was recorded at Ellesmere Island.

7. Parts of Russia are famous for their coldness. A temperature taken at Oymyakon in Siberia.

8. Seriously cold temperature taken at Vostok in Antarctica.

B

1. How much colder was Oymyakon than Sodankyla?
2. How much hotter was Death Valley than Cordoba?
3. How much below freezing point was the temperature at Ellesmere Island?
4. What is the difference in temperature between the hottest and coldest places?

C

Here are some winter temperatures taken in the UK.

London	–3°C
Edinburgh	–5°C
Cardiff	2°C
Belfast	3°C

1. How much colder was London than Belfast?
2. How much warmer was Cardiff than Edinburgh?
3. The temperature in London dropped by 2°. Write the new temperature.
4. The temperature in Edinburgh rose by 3°. Write the new temperature.

D

Make a chart to show some temperatures in different cities.

Information

Multiplication square

x	1	2	3	4	5	6	7	8	9	10
1	1	2	3	4	5	6	7	8	9	10
2	2	4	6	8	10	12	14	16	18	20
3	3	6	9	12	15	18	21	24	27	30
4	4	8	12	16	20	24	28	32	36	40
5	5	10	15	20	25	30	35	40	45	50
6	6	12	18	24	30	36	42	48	54	60
7	7	14	21	28	35	42	49	56	63	70
8	8	16	24	32	40	48	56	64	72	80
9	9	18	27	36	45	54	63	72	81	90
10	10	20	30	40	50	60	70	80	90	100

Square and triangle numbers to 100

Square numbers	1	4	9	16	25	36	49	64	81	100			
Triangle numbers	1	3	6	10	15	21	28	36	45	55	66	78	91

Measurements

10 mm = 1 cm
100 cm = 1 m
1000 mm = 1 m
1000 m = 1 km

1000 g = 1 kg
1000 kg = 1 tonne

10 ml = 1 cl
100 cl = 1 l
1000 ml = 1 l